net into two straight angle triangles, each of which is kept respectively at right angles to each side of the oblong net aforesaid by means of loops and strings, and is fixed to pegs driven in the ground.

The large oblong net forms the dividing wall of the court, and the triangular net the wings or side walls thereof, whilst the floor is marked out by paint, coloured cord, or tape into "in" and "out" courts, serving as crease, right and left courts, and boundaries. By this simple apparatus a portable court is obtained by means of which the old game of tennis, which has always been an indoor amusement, and which few can enjoy on account of the great expense of building a brick court, may be made an outdoor one, and placed within the reach of all, as the above described portable court can be erected in a few minutes on a lawn, on ice, or in any suitable sized space either in or out of doors.

WITHDRAWN

SPECIFICATION in pursuance of the conditions of the Letters Patent, filed by the said Walter Clopton Wingfield in the Great Seal Patent Office on the 22nd August 1874.

TO ALL TO WHOM THESE PRESENTS SHALL COME, I, WALTER CLOPTON WINGFIELD, of Belgrave Road, Pimlico, in the County of Middlesex, send greeting.

WHEREAS Her most Excellent Majesty Queen Victoria, by Her Letters Patent, bearing date the Twenty-third day of February, in the year of our Lord One thousand eight hundred and seventy-four, in the thirty-seventh year of Her reign, did, for Herself, Her heirs and successors, give and grant unto me, the said Walter Clopton Wingfield, Her special licence that I, the said Walter Clopton Wingfield, my executors, administrators, and assigns, or such others as I, the said Walter Clopton Wingfield, my executors, administrators, and assigns, should at any time agree with, and no others, from time to time and at all times thereafter during the term therein expressed, should and lawfully might make, use, exercise, and vend, within the United Kingdom of Great Britain and Ireland, the Channel Islands, and Isle of Man, an Invention for "A NEW AND IMPROVED PORTABLE COURT FOR PLAYING THE ANCIENT GAME OF TENNIS," upon the condition (amongst others) that I, the said Walter Clopton Wingfield, my executors or administrators, by an instrument in writing under my, or their, or one of their hands and seals, should particularly describe and ascertain the nature of the said Invention, and in what manner the same is to be performed, and cause the same to be filed in the Great Seal Patent Office within six calendar months next and immediately after the date of said Letters Patent.

D1205584

(Continued on back endpaper)

BK   796.342   T137T
TENNIS TACTICS : SINGLES AND DOUBLES
                                    /TALBERT, W
1   C1983   14.95   FV

3000 631217 30018
St. Louis Community College

796.342 T137t   FV
TALBERT
TENNIS TACTICS : SINGLES AND
DOUBLES

                              14.95

St. Louis Community College

Library

5801 Wilson Avenue
St. Louis, Missouri 63110

TENNIS TACTICS

BY THE SAME AUTHORS:

The Game of Singles in Tennis
The Game of Doubles in Tennis
Stroke Production in the Game of Tennis

TENNIS TACTICS

SINGLES AND DOUBLES

WILLIAM F. TALBERT

AND

BRUCE S. OLD

DRAWINGS BY KATHARINE D. OLD

1817

HARPER & ROW, PUBLISHERS • NEW YORK

CAMBRIDGE, PHILADELPHIA, SAN FRANCISCO,
LONDON, MEXICO CITY, SÀO PAULO, SYDNEY

Grateful acknowledgment is made for permission to reprint drawings on page 39 by Ed Vebell, courtesy of *Sports Illustrated*. © 1957 Time Inc.

TENNIS TACTICS. Copyright © 1983 by William F. Talbert and Bruce S. Old. All rights reserved. Printed in the United States of America. No part of this book may be used or reproduced in any manner whatsoever without written permission except in the case of brief quotations embodied in critical articles and reviews. For information address Harper & Row, Publishers, Inc., 10 East 53rd Street, New York, N.Y. 10022. Published simultaneously in Canada by Fitzhenry & Whiteside Limited, Toronto.

FIRST EDITION

Designer: Helene Berinsky

Library of Congress Cataloging in Publication Data

Talbert, William F.
  Tennis tactics.

  1. Tennis. I. Old, Bruce S.   II. Title.
GV995.T33   1983   796.342′2   82–48137
ISBN 0-06-015111-0

83 84 85 86 87 10 9 8 7 6 5 4 3 2 1

to Nancy and Bunny

CONTENTS

ILLUSTRATIONS

TABLES

FOREWORD

It seems fitting that Bill Talbert and Bruce Old would come out with another tennis instructional book—this time on *Tennis Tactics*. Their book on doubles remains the definitive opus on the subject.

Tennis Tactics has something in it for everybody. No one will want to read it all at once; but it is so good that the urge to explore it thoroughly will be hard to suppress.

The great majority of tennis books have concern on stroke production. With 30 million players around now, most people seem to know how to hit a forehand and a backhand but few know the why and wherefores.

I would like to suggest a fun way of getting through *Tennis Tactics*. First, read through a couple of sections that interest you most. Then sit down and watch the next televised tennis event like, say, the U.S. Open and try to connect what you have absorbed in *Tennis Tactics* with what you see the pros do. You will be amazed at the similarities, or better yet, you will understand why certain pros would do well to read *Tennis Tactics* themselves.

For the beginner who wants the strategy at his fingertips one day, to the advanced player who's looking for that extra edge, *Tennis Tactics* answers the most-asked questions.

One last note: Neither *Tennis Tactics* nor any other book can replace lessons with real, live, experienced teaching professionals. In the meantime, get your racket back, follow through, and have a good time.

Arthur R. Ashe Jr.

PREFACE

The sport of tennis requires an exacting combination of intelligence, confidence, and skill. The two games of singles and doubles in tennis demand widely differing tactics. This basic book by Bill Talbert and Bruce Old provides, for the first time under one cover, invaluable instruction in the unique strategies of both singles and doubles. I think it can be of practical assistance to you as a reference book throughout your tennis-playing life. I commend it to you for repeated study.

Chris Evert Lloyd

TENNIS TACTICS

1

INTRODUCTION

This book has a unique objective. Unlike any others ever written on tennis, it is devoted to presenting under one cover a detailed exposition of the basic tactics employed in winning tennis for the games of both singles and doubles. The presentation is meant to be simple, yet authoritative. It is aimed at the tournament player as well as the novice, young and old, and both sexes. It should also prove invaluable to instructors and coaches. But, above all, this book is designed to increase the enjoyment of the great game of tennis by players and spectators alike, through increasing their skill and understanding.

Why are tactics important? One former world champion stated it this way: "Perfect style, inexhaustible stamina, even the best strokes are of no avail if the brain that governs the hand is not taking stock of strategical positions and planning moves by which winning coups may be achieved." A number of variables interact to complicate tactical decisions. The speed, height, spin, angular direction, and depth of the ball; relative court positions of the players: stroke likes and dislikes of the opponents; speed and stamina of the contestants; wind, sun, and temperature; and court surface characteristics—all combine to present the striking and receiving players with an unending number of situations to be sorted out before the proper tactical answers can be determined. The answer must include how to diagnose the direction and type of shot being directed at you; where to position yourself to make your reply; where to elect to place your return; what type of stroke, speed, and

Figure 1

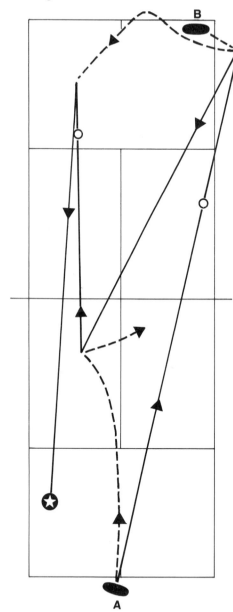

DIAGRAM METHOD

This figure illustrates the method used to diagram points in this book. It also serves to show how two mistakes by player A cost him this particular point.

Player A serves deep to the backhand of player B and then rushes to net to volley the return. Receiver B hits a cross-court backhand return of service, which server A volleys back. However, he makes his first tactical mistake by hitting the volley too shallow. This gives receiver B, who had retreated to the normal defensive base-line position, an opportunity to move forward and take the offense. Server A then moves properly to his right to cover a possible cross-court return. But he makes his second mistake by overcommitting and continuing to run beyond the center line. While moving forward, a glance by receiver B assesses the situation and he decides there is room to slip a passing shot behind player A before he can regain balance and reverse direction. As shown, this tactic results in a well-deserved placement.

All tactical maneuvers which are diagrammed in this book were taken from actual points played in tournament matches.

Symbols Used in Diagrams

Solid oval denotes tennis player, and letter identifies the player.

Dashed line shows the path of player moving from one position to another, the arrow indicating direction.

Solid line shows flight of tennis ball, the arrow indicating direction.

Dash-dot line shows a lob.

Small circle shows bounce point of ball.

Large circle shows aim point for a shot.

Circle with star shows aim point for placement.

spin to employ; and where and when to position yourself to handle the anticipated answering stroke by your opponent. The time allotted for the brain to assess the situation and compute a proper tactical reply is often less than half a second!

It is apparent that the making of tactical decisions in tennis must be so instantaneous that the player has to develop an instinct for diagnosing the possibilities at a glance, and then making the most effective response. For this reason, this book should be read and reread until the choice of proper tactics becomes essentially instinctive or automatic. Extensive practice and tournament play will be necessary to perfect your employment of sound tactics.

In order to gather information for this book the authors have studied many singles matches between the great men players over the past twenty-five years, from Gonzalez, Rosewall, and Laver to Connors, Borg, and McEnroe, and doubles teams from Newcombe-Roche, Hewitt-McMillan, and Lutz-Smith to Fleming-McEnroe. Also the recent great women singles players were similarly studied, including Margaret Smith Court, Billie Jean King, Chris Evert Lloyd, Evonne Goolagong Cawley, Martina Navratilova, and Tracy Austin. And the doubles tactics of Court, King, Navratilova, and partners were reviewed. The analyses have been accomplished by recording data in person at matches, and by the use of numerous television tapes of tournaments, which were played and replayed many times for study. Thus, our statements about tactics employed are based upon many thousands of actual points. For comparison purposes, some data were also collected from matches played by the less expert players of local club caliber.

Finally, we also reviewed the tennis literature to search out additional information. Included in this were the three previous, widely read books by the authors.*

To assist the reader, a number of diagrams and drawings have been utilized to illustrate clearly the tactical situations facing the players in selected points from actual matches. A typical example of a diagram is given in Figure 1 in order to present the method and the symbols utilized.

---

* William F. Talbert and Bruce S. Old, *The Game of Doubles in Tennis*. New York: Lippincott, 1956, 1968, 1977; William F. Talbert and Bruce S. Old, *The Game of Singles in Tennis*. New York: Lippincott, 1962, 1977; William F. Talbert and Bruce S. Old, *Stroke Production in the Game of Tennis*. New York: Lippincott, 1971.

2

BRIEF HISTORY

Tennis as we know it today began in England in 1873 with the invention of lawn tennis by Major Walter Clopton Wingfield. His description of the game was first recorded for some of his friends in a booklet, *The Major's Game of Lawn Tennis*—dedicated to the party assembled at Nantclwyd in December 1873. His unique summary of the game is worth quoting.

> The Game of Tennis may be traced back to the days of the ancient Greeks, under the name of σφαιριστικὴ. It was subsequently played by the Romans under the name of "Pila." Court tennis was the fashionable pastime of the nobles of France, during the reign of Charles V, and it was in vogue in England as early as Henry III, and is described by Gregory as "one of the most ancient games in Christendom." Henry V, Henry VII, and Henry VIII were all court tennis players, and it has only now died out owing to the difficulties of the game, and the expense of erecting courts. All these difficulties have been surmounted by the inventor of "Lawn Tennis," which has all the interest of "tennis," and has the advantage that it may be played in the open air in any weather by people of any age and both sexes. In a hard frost the nets may be erected on the ice, and the players being equipped with skates, the Games assumes a new feature, and gives an opening for the exhibition of much grace and science.
>
> Croquet, which of late has monopolized the attention of the public, lacks the healthy and manly excitement of "Lawn Tennis." Moreover, this game has the advantage that, while an adept at tennis or racquets would rapidly become a really scientific player, the merest tyro can learn it in five minutes sufficiently well for all practical purposes.

Wingfield could not resist adding some advice on tactics: Hit your ball gently, and look well before striking, so as to place it in the corner most remote from your adversary. A great deal of side can be imparted to the ball by the proper touch, which, together with a nice appreciation of strength, adds much to the delicacy and science of the game.

Major Wingfield applied for a patent on the game February 23, 1874, and was awarded Letters Patent No. 685 for "A Portable Court for Playing Tennis." The game became popular the world over, quite rapidly largely because of its enthusiastic adoption by the British Army as a barracks exercise.

Tennis was brought to the United States in 1874 by Miss Mary Outerbridge of Staten Island, who acquired the equipment from some British Army officers in Bermuda. It spread to India in 1875, to Germany in 1876, to France in 1877, and to Australia in 1878.

The first tennis tournament was organized at Wimbledon, England, in 1877. It has been played ever since, except for wartime interruptions, and its rich tradition makes the All-England Tennis Championships such a drawing card for players throughout the world that it is generally considered the greatest tournament.

The second most important tournament is the United States National Championship, which was first played in 1881 at Newport, Rhode Island. It later moved to Philadelphia and to Forest Hills, and currently is held at Flushing Meadow, New York, under the name U.S. Open Tennis Championships. The other two tournaments which go to make up the Grand Slam of tennis are the French and Australian championships.

Only two men players have ever won all four of these famous singles championships in the same year:—J. Donald Budge of the United States in 1938, and Rodney Laver of Australia in 1962 and 1969. And only one men's doubles team has won all four: Frank Sedgman and Kenneth McGregor of Australia in 1951. In mixed doubles, Ken Fletcher and Margaret Smith Court of Australia gained a Grand Slam in 1963. The only two women who have pulled off a singles Grand Slam were Maureen Connolly of the United States in 1953 and Margaret Smith Court of Australia in 1970.

The records of the outstanding singles and doubles players of the past forty years are shown in Tables 1, 2, 3, 4, and 5. To measure the performance of individuals, we have chosen the Wimbledon and U.S. championships and the top professional ranking as the best three indicators of excellence. Professional tennis became an important aspect of

TABLE 1

Outstanding Men Singles Players 1940 to Date

TOURNAMENT AND YEAR OF VICTORY

Name and Nationality	Wimbledon	United States	Top-Ranking Professionals
John A. Kramer (U.S.)	47	46, 47	48, 49, 50, 51, 52
Richard A. Gonzalez (U.S.)		48, 49	53, 54, 55, 56, 57, 58, 59, 60, 61
Rodney Laver (A.)	61, 62, 68, 69	62, 69	65, 66, 67, 68, 69
John Newcombe (A.)	67, 70, 71	67, 73	
James S. Connors (U.S.)	74, 82	74, 76, 78, 82	74, 76, 78, 82
Bjorn Borg (Sw.)	76, 77, 78, 79, 80		77, 79, 80
John McEnroe (U.S.)	81	79, 80, 81	81

TABLE 2

Outstanding Men Doubles Players 1940 to Date

TOURNAMENT AND YEAR OF VICTORY

Name and Nationality	Wimbledon	United States	Top-Ranking Professionals
John E. Bromwich (A.) and Adrian K. Quist (A.)	50	39	
John E. Bromwich (A.) and William Sidwell (A.)		49	
John E. Bromwich (A.) and Frank Sedgman (A.)	48	50	
Gardnar Mulloy (U.S.) and William F. Talbert (U.S.)		42, 45, 46, 48	
Gardnar Mulloy (U.S.) and Budge Patty (U.S.)	57		
Frank Sedgman (A.) and John E. Bromwich (A.)	48	50	
Frank Sedgman (A.) and Kenneth McGregor (A.)	51, 52	51	
Roy Emerson (A.) and Neale A. Fraser (A.)	59, 61	59, 60	
Roy Emerson (A.) and Rodney Laver (A.)	71		
Roy Emerson (A.) and Fred Stolle (A.)		65, 66	

| | TOURNAMENT AND YEAR OF VICTORY | | |
| | | | Top-Ranking |
Name and Nationality	Wimbledon	United States	Professionals
John Newcombe (A.) and Tony Roche (A.)	65, 68, 69, 70, 74	67	
John Newcombe (A.) and Ken Fletcher (A.)	66		
John Newcombe (A.) and Roger Taylor (A.)		71	
John Newcombe (A.) and Owen Davidson (A.)		73	
Robert Hewitt (S.A.) and Fred Stolle (A.)	62, 64		
Robert Hewitt (S.A.) and Frew McMillan (S.A.)	67, 72, 78	77	
Robert Lutz (U.S.) and Stanley R. Smith (U.S.)		68, 74, 78, 80	68, 78, 80
John McEnroe (U.S.) and Peter Fleming (U.S.)	79, 81	79, 81	81

TABLE 3

Outstanding Women Singles Players 1940 to Date

| | TOURNAMENT AND YEAR OF VICTORY | | |
| | | | Top-Ranking |
Name and Nationality	Wimbledon	United States	Professionals
Pauline Betz (U.S.)	46	42, 43, 44, 46	
Margaret Osborne duPont (U.S.)	47	48, 49, 50	
A. Louise Brough (U.S.)	48, 49, 50, 55	47	
Maureen Connolly (U.S.)	52, 53, 54	51, 52, 53	
Maria E. Bueno (Brazil)	59, 60, 64	59, 63, 64, 66	
Margaret Smith Court (A.)	63, 65, 70	62, 65, 68, 69, 70, 73	73
Billie Jean King (U.S.)	66, 67, 68, 72, 73, 75	67, 71, 72, 74	72
Chris Evert Lloyd (U.S.)	74, 76, 81	75, 76, 77, 78, 80, 82	74, 75, 76, 77, 78, 80, 81
Martina Navratilova (U.S.)	78, 79, 82		
Tracy Austin (U.S.)		79, 81	82

TABLE 4

Outstanding Women Doubles Players 1940 to Date

	TOURNAMENT AND YEAR OF VICTORY	
Name and Nationality	*Wimbledon*	*United States*
Margaret Osborne duPont (U.S.) and Sarah Palfrey (U.S.)		41
Margaret Osborne duPont (U.S.) and A. Louise Brough (U.S.)	46, 48, 49, 50, 54	42, 43, 44, 45, 46, 47 48, 49, 50, 55, 56, 57
Doris Hart (U.S.) and Shirley Fry (U.S.)	51, 52, 53	51, 52, 53, 54
Darlene R. Hard (U.S.) and Althea Gibson (U.S.)	57	
Darlene R. Hard (U.S.) and Jeanne Arth (U.S.)	59	58, 59
Darlene R. Hard (U.S.) and Maria E. Bueno (Br.)	60, 63	60, 62
Darlene R. Hard (U.S.) and Lesley Turner (A.)		61
Darlene R. Hard (U.S.) and Françoise Durr (Fr.)		69
Maria E. Bueno (Brazil) and Althea Gibson (U.S.)	58	
Maria E. Bueno (Br.) and Darlene R. Hard (U.S.)	60, 63	60, 62
Maria E. Bueno (Br.) and Billie Jean King (U.S.)	65	
Maria E. Bueno (Br.) and Nancy Richey (U.S.)	66	66
Maria E. Bueno (Br.) and Margaret Smith Court (A.)		68
Billie Jean King (U.S.) and Karen H. Susman (U.S.)	61, 62	64
Billie Jean King (U.S.) and Maria E. Bueno (Br.)	65	
Billie Jean King (U.S.) and Rosemary Casals (U.S.)	67, 68, 70, 71, 73	67, 74
Billie Jean King (U.S.) and Betty Stove (Neth.)	72	
Billie Jean King (U.S.) and Martina Navratilova (U.S.)	79	78, 80
Margaret Court Smith (A.) and Robyn Ebbern (A.)		63
Margaret Court Smith (A.) and Lesley Turner (A.)	64	
Margaret Court Smith (A.) and Maria E. Bueno (Br.)		68

	TOURNAMENT AND YEAR OF VICTORY	
Name and Nationality	Wimbledon	United States
Margaret Court Smith (A.) and Virginia Wade (U.K.)		73, 75
Margaret Court Smith (A.) and Judy T. Dalton (A.)	69	70
Martina Navratilova (U.S.) and Chris Evert Lloyd (U.S.)	76	
Martina Navratilova (U.S.) and Betty Stove (Neth.)		77
Martina Navratilova (U.S.) and Billie Jean King (U.S.)	79	78, 80
Martina Navratilova (U.S.) and Pam Shriver (U.S.)	81, 82	

TABLE 5

Outstanding Mixed Doubles Players 1940 to Date

	TOURNAMENT AND YEAR OF VICTORY	
Name and Nationality	Wimbledon	United States
Margaret Osborne duPont (U.S.) and William F. Talbert (U.S.)		43, 44, 45, 46
Margaret Osborne duPont (U.S.) and Kenneth McGregor (A.)		50
Margaret Osborne duPont (U.S.) and Kenneth Rosewall (A.)		56
Margaret Osborne duPont (U.S.) and Neale Fraser (A.)	62	58, 59, 60
A. Louise Brough (U.S.) and Frederick E. Schroeder (U.S.)		42
A. Louise Brough (U.S.) and John Bromwich (A.)	47, 48	48
A. Louise Brough (U.S.) and Thomas P. Brown (U.S.)	46	48
A. Louise Brough (U.S.) and Eric Sturgess (S.A.)	50	49
Doris Hart (U.S.) and Frank Sedgman (A.)	51, 52	51, 52
Doris Hart (U.S.) and E. Victor Seixas (U.S.)	53, 54, 55, 56	53, 54, 55
Margaret Smith Court (A.) and Robert Mark (A.)		61

	TOURNAMENT AND YEAR OF VICTORY	
Name and Nationality	*Wimbledon*	*United States*
Margaret Smith Court (A.) and Fred Stolle (A.)		62, 65
Margaret Smith Court (A.) and Ken Fletcher (A.)	63, 65, 66, 68	63
Margaret Smith Court (A.) and John Newcombe (A.)		64
Margaret Smith Court (A.) and Martin Riessen (U.S.)	75	69, 70, 72
Billie Jean King (U.S.) and Owen Davidson (A.)	67, 71, 73, 74	67, 71, 73
Billie Jean King (U.S.) and Phil Dent (A.)		76

the game about forty years ago when many of the top amateurs turned professional. However, until about 1968 they were not allowed to participate in the still amateur Wimbledon and U.S. championships. Since then all the important tournaments worldwide are open in nature and welcome both amateur and professional entrants.

Particular attention is called to Table 5 on mixed doubles champions. It goes to prove that the outcome of a mixed doubles match depends almost entirely on the skill of the lady member. Over the years the top women's doubles players have dominated the mixed championships playing with various male partners. Men winners the world over are warned to remember and acknowledge this fact!

3

THE GAMES

The games of singles and doubles in tennis are similar in a number of ways, but entirely distinctive in many others. Therefore, it is necessary in this book to differentiate clearly between the proper tactics to employ in each game.

Tennis is an intellectual game of high order and great complexity because of the unending variety of situations which face the players. Nevertheless, it is possible to simplify your play by developing a sound knowledge and understanding of the fundamentals. Such comprehension should permit you to play the proper shot, in the most effective manner, at the right moment, almost automatically or intuitively. This is certainly what the champions almost always do, which explains why some do not realize they are thinking on each stroke. They exhibit an uncanny instinct for making the correct shot—but do not forget that this ability to solve a variety of tennis styles was developed through many hours of practice, coaching, study, and tournament experience.

There may appear to be exceptions to the rule that champions are great tacticians. From time to time there arrives on the scene a player who is so outstanding he overpowers all the opposition by the very severity of his or her strokes. But any such dominance is usually short-lived. Either age slows down the forcing shots, or a brilliant new tactician emerges who can pick the champion apart with a carefully selected assortment of soft, spinning shots which blunt the attacking weapons. The smart former champion then has to learn how to alter his tactics in order to regain his capability of winning.

Thus we return to the major purpose of this book, which is to provide an exposition of sound tennis tactics. Tactics are defined as "the science and art of disposing and maneuvering forces in combat," or "the art or skill of employing available means to accomplish an end." A reader who learns to make most of the basic plays essentially by habit can then concentrate on the more subtle factors. You will discover this will have a tremendous effect on your ability to overcome your own weaknesses and to exploit those of your opponent.

In this chapter we will attempt to present overall pictures of the games of singles and doubles to set the stage for later details.

Before launching into the characteristics of the games, something must be said about types of tennis courts, since the various surfaces have a marked effect on determining style of play. It may seem unbelievable, but a change of a small fraction of a second in speed of ball bounce makes a significant difference in the tactics which should be employed. On hard, fast courts the ball tends to skid low, whereas on soft, slow courts the ball digs in and bounces higher. Tennis courts can be ranked in terms of speed as follows: board, hard court (cement or asphalt), grass, composition, and, finally, clay, the slowest of all. For all practical purposes, a dividing line can be made at the point of grass, as all matches played on grass or above can be categorized as played on fast courts. Most of the important tournaments worldwide are played on fast courts. These favor the so-called "big game" in singles, which utilizes tactics of powerful serve and volley rather than base-line exchange. On the slower composition and clay courts the defender has the added time to take another step or two to retrieve the higher-bouncing ball. This seemingly small change alters substantially the tactics and the strokes which win points, as shown in Table 6. Not even the best of the big servers can continually attack the net and volley with success on a slow court. Instead, long base-line rallies become the standard arena for determination of winning maneuvers. In doubles the court surface has much less effect on tactics, as the importance of gaining the net position is paramount irrespective of surface—winning strokes are similar on slow or fast courts (see Table 7).

In studying winning types of strokes it is important to take into account the frequency with which the stroke is utilized. When that is done the "lethality," or ratio of winning shots to total shots as compared with other strokes, can be determined. These data for singles and doubles fast-court play are presented in Table 8. The fascinating finding which

TABLE 6

Percent Frequency of Stroke Utilization and Winners in Men's Singles

	First Serve	Second Serve	Return of Service	First Volley	Later Volley	Over-head	Ground Stroke at Net	Passing Shot	Base-Line Rally	Lob
Fast Court										
Frequency	24.5	13	25	18	7	1	0.5	9	0	2
Winners	23	10	21	17	13	3	1	9	0	3
Slow Court										
Winners	17	6	15	2	12	3	3	18	20	3

TABLE 7

Percent Frequency of Stroke Utilization and Winners in Men's Doubles

	First Serve	Second Serve	Return of Service	Other Ground Strokes	Volley	Overhead	Lob
Fast Court							
Frequency	23	7	22.5	10	26.5	6	5
Winners	18	1	12	12	41	14	2

TABLE 8

Relative Probability of Winning a Point with a Given Type of Stroke Considering the Frequency of Use

SINGLES		DOUBLES	
Stroke	Lethality	Stroke	Lethality
Overhead	3.9	Overhead	14.5
Ground stroke at net	2.6	Volley	9.5
Later volley	2.4	Passing shot	7.5
Lob	1.9	First service	5
Passing shot	1.3	Return of service	3
First service	1.2	Lob	2.5
First volley	1.2	Second service	1
Return of service	1.1		
Second service	1.0	(basis of comparison)	

emerges from this table is that the net territory in both singles and doubles is confirmed as the best attacking area.

An overall examination of the games of tennis shows some generic similarities and some basic differences between the singles and doubles games.

First, the similarities.

TENNIS IS AVAILABLE TO ALL

Since the singles court is only 78 x 27 feet and the doubles court is only slightly larger at 78 x 36 feet, little room is required to build either outdoor or indoor facilities. As a result, both public and private courts exist all over the world, and rental fees for use are usually reasonable. Also, the athletic clothes and equipment required are inexpensive and easy to transport. All of these factors combine to make tennis available to millions of participants ranging from eight to eighty years, including both sexes, in essentially every nation around the globe. The smooth, rhythmic, intensely athletic nature of the game makes tennis of absorbing interest to both players and spectators. For these reasons, tennis is one of the most popular of all sports.

TENNIS REQUIRES SKILL AND SPEED

During a match many tennis balls are struck at speeds of about 100 miles per hour, which means they would travel the entire length of the court in just over half a second. The receiver of such blistering strokes must be able to anticipate in which direction to move, but then has time to dash only five to six feet in the proper direction in order to intercept the fastest balls. To make matters worse, many balls bounce erratically, particularly on grass surfaces. In most three-set matches, depending on the court-surface speed, the ball is struck by each player from 300 to 1800 times. As a result, tennis, unlike many sports, runs true to form. After all, stroke-production technique, style, balance, footwork, court coverage, anticipation, timing, shot selection, and placement capabilities are bound to assert themselves over Lady Luck during an extended match. Entailing high-speed ball and player movement within a court of limited size, tennis can truly be described as a game of tenths of seconds and tenths of inches.

ANTICIPATION

Tennis is such a fast game that to cover the court to make either ground-stroke or volley returns is often impossible unless the receiver can anticipate the type, direction, and speed of stroke about to be delivered by the striker. The receiver has to be moving in the right direction at the proper split second if he is to have a chance.

The art of anticipation has four parts. First, you must assess from the type and placement of your own shot what type and direction of return to expect. Second, you have to study the stroking techniques of your opponent in order to discover his style, technique, idiosyncrasies, and favorite shots under various tactical conditions. Third, you need to concentrate on the giveaway motions of the opponent striking the ball. This entails watching, not the ball, but the position of the striker's feet, body, racket arm, backswing, and racket head as it meets the ball. While this may seem very complicated, after some practice you can learn to diagnose the intentions of the striker with respect to type, direction, and speed of shot at a glance. And, fourth, you (and your partner, if playing doubles) must shift position to meet the expected return. Any shift has to be timed exactly, as a premature move might permit the striker to change direction and win the point by hitting behind you.

DETERMINATION

Closely linked to the requirements of concentration and courage as a must in top tennis players is the invaluable asset called determination. It is that hard-to-define extra in the makeup of a player which permits him to lift his game at the precise moment of crisis in order to win. It is a rare quality that stamps many local as well as national champions—it divides the winners from those who just get close.

Determination is much more than just trying hard for each point in a match. It also entails the willingness to face untold hours of practice to improve your techniques, the courage to come from behind, and the ability to control the delicate balance between having confidence, which is essential, and overconfidence, which is poisonous, to top performance.

Desire leads to victory through the type of tenacious court coverage that ultimately discourages the opposition.

SPORTSMANSHIP

More than most sports, tennis demands and breeds sportsmanship. An important contributing factor is that the game is normally played without either an umpire or linesmen. For that reason, players must call all balls or rule infractions on their side of the net. It is a firm, unwritten rule that one always gives the opponent the benefit of the doubt on close decisions. In fact, during informal matches it often happens that the striker will claim that his shot was out, after a generous receiver has already ruled otherwise. When players cannot agree, a let is called and the point is played over again. Such actions represent a fine exhibition of fair play which is customary in few sports.

The traditions of the game also call for courtesy, no alibis, and a minimum of temperament display. While some dramatic exceptions have occurred in recent widely televised matches, the cult of true sportsmanship is bound to prevail over time because of the overwhelming demands of spectators, participants, and officials of the sports-governing bodies which regulate the great sport of tennis around the world.

And now to mention some of the differences between the games of singles and doubles.

SINGLES REQUIRES GREATER STAMINA

Singles demands more stamina than doubles, as one player must cover the entire court. In fact, the game has been described by one of the greatest singles players of all time as "putting the athlete under the hardest physical, mental, and nervous strain of any game played by mankind." The truth of this statement is attested to by the fact that few men or women beyond the age of thirty have ever won a major singles championship. This age limit for supremacy is younger than in many sports often considered to be more rugged—such as football, hockey, basketball, boxing, and soccer. The stamina requirements in singles spring not just from the two to four hours of hard running, quick starts and stops, changes of direction, and stretching, but also from the generalship requirements with the accompanying strain of numerous and continuous decisions which must be made within a split-second time allowance throughout the match. All the time, a player has to study the style, strokes, and psychology of the opponent in order to learn his strengths and weaknesses and anticipate his moves. There is a continual duel of speed, spin, change of pace, depth and angles, and surprise in order to exploit one another's vulnerabilities. To emerge victorious requires tremendous and undivided powers of concentration and imagination. No wonder tennis players are often exhausted after a match, and find it very difficult to stay at top form throughout a large tournament.

DOUBLES REQUIRES TEAMWORK

Unlike singles, doubles is a team game. It is not just singles with two players on each side of the court—it is a game entirely by itself. Individual brilliance must be submerged, and coordinated team effort emphasized. Hours of practicing together, learning one another's games, planning strategy and tactics, establishing optimum court positions for varying situations, studying possible weaknesses in the games of the opposition, encouraging and steadying one's partner by "talking it up" when the going is difficult—all these and more are essential to superior doubles teamwork.

Most great doubles teams have been made up of players with complementary styles. They are composed of a play maker combined with a power player. The play makers have been masters of doubles who utilized every bit of tactical finesse, anticipation, stroke variety, spins, fakes, teasers, and well-planned maneuvers to force the opponents to leave an opening or to make a weak return. At that split second the power player must move in to blast the winner. He has usually been a rangy individual with great speed, superb timing, a powerful volley, and a devastating overhead. Even the best of such perfect pairings require some years of playing together to conquer the complexities of teamwork. As seen in Tables 2 and 4, the doubles masters manage to win with several different power players as partners. Selecting a partner who combines well with your style is important for any player interested in tournament tennis.

OFFENSIVE PATTERNS DIFFER

In singles on a fast court the "big game" of power serve followed in to net for a strong offensive first volley wins about 50 percent of all points. Later volleys and overheads made because of the advantage gained through the attacking net position bring to over 60 percent the total points won using the offensive style of singles.

However, as earlier pointed out in Table 6, a slow-court bounce takes so much off the effectiveness of the big serve that the game of singles changes dramatically. The serve now wins only about 17 percent of points, and the first volley, which even the best servers can seldom attempt for fear of being passed, wins only 2 percent. The pattern of play changes to an exchange of base-line drives with occasional forays to the net when weak returns present an opportunity. As a result, about 45 percent of points are won on ground strokes and 12 percent on later volleys.

By way of contrast, doubles is essentially the same game irrespective of court surface. Net play so dominates doubles, winning about 55 percent of all points (Table 7), that the server must take net on both first and second serves on all court surfaces.

APPEAL TO PLAYERS AND SPECTATORS

The comparative appeal of singles and doubles usually resolves itself into a matter of personal preference.

For the players, singles certainly represents the greater glory, since the honor and public recognition attached to winning a key championship bring about lifelong satisfaction. Also, singles provides more exercise. And many dedicated spectators prefer watching the tingling drama of a duel between two top players who must call upon the ultimate in stamina and courage in order to determine final superiority.

Doubles has its own special qualities. The players must employ a greater variety of strokes, resourcefulness, and also teamwork during a continuing barrage of rapid, point-blank exchanges. For sheer enjoyment, thrills, and satisfaction the players find the four-handed game to represent the art of tennis ingenuity at its highest. And a good portion of sophisticated spectators concurs that there is more excitement and fun in watching doubles played by two competent, evenly matched teams.

REMARKS ON THE FUNDAMENTALS OF STROKE PRODUCTION

This book is aimed at understanding tactics and not at teaching stroke production, which encompasses how to hit the various strokes used in tennis. However, some readers would no doubt welcome a few words on how to master the strokes, without which one cannot proceed to employ proper tactics. The best way to learn, of course, is to seek instruction from a competent coach or professional.

The first thing to consider is how to grip the tennis racket. We have selected for illustrative purposes in Figures 2, 3, and 4 the grips employed by several great players: William T. Tilden, J. Donald Budge, Rodney Laver, and Chris Evert Lloyd.

The two most popular grips are the Eastern, which has been employed by many champions in addition to Tilden and Budge, and the Continental, which is used by such players as Laver, McEnroe, and Billie Jean King. The Western grip, which is used for the top-spin forehand by Bjorn Borg, has the hand a quarter turn more to the right than the Eastern forehand. One of the more recent grips is the two-handed backhand, which has been popularized by Chris Evert Lloyd, Borg, and others.

The Eastern forehand grip is often described as "shaking hands with the racket," with the V between the thumb and forefinger pointing almost directly at the right shoulder (see Figure 2). The backhand grip is rotated about a quarter turn to the left so that the V is now pointing over the left shoulder and the thumb is in the back of the racket. Both

Figure 2: Eastern Grip (Righthander)

of these methods of holding the racket are "strong" grips, in that you can easily resist a friend who attempts to push the racket head against your grasp. The backhand grip with thumb slightly downward is the preferred Eastern serving grip.

Figure 3 illustrates the Continental grip of Rod Laver, which has the advantage of being appropriate, without any correcting rotation, for all strokes. It is not quite as strong as the Eastern forehand grip, as the hand is about one-eighth turn more on top of the racket. This is definitely the preferred grip for volleying, because the same grip is used for forehands, backhands, and overheads, so that no time is lost at point blank range in making rotational adjustments.

Figure 3: Continental Grip (Lefthander)

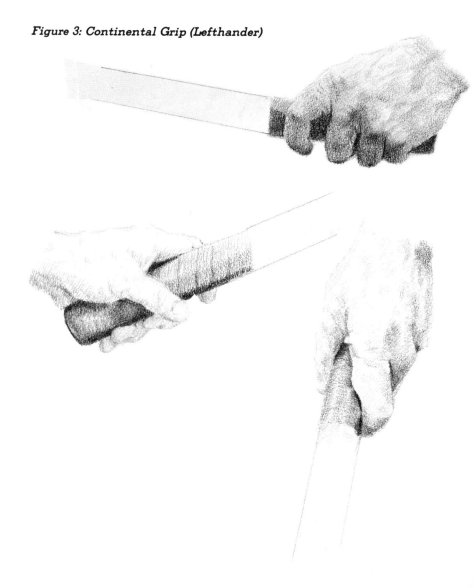

The two-handed grip, shown in Figure 4, has been used from time to time in the past but was not popular until recent years. Chris Evert Lloyd first used it when she was so young she had a difficult time controlling the heavy racket. As she perfected the grip, which is made up of two Eastern forehand grips, she realized the advantages it provided in deception. The ball can be directed down the line or cross court, hard or soft, at the last moment, so that it is difficult to read. Many ranking men as well as women now employ this grip.

Of great significance is that these popular grips permit the player to impart purposeful spin to the tennis ball, the flight of which, like many other similar objects, is aerodynamically controlled by such spin. For

Figure 4: Two-handed Backhand Grip (Righthander)

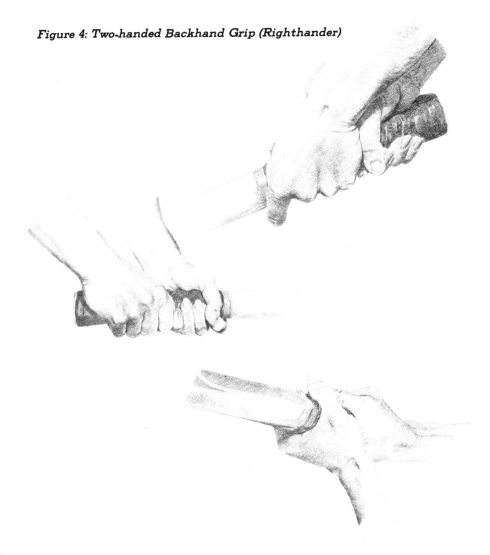

example, the reader undoubtedly recognizes that guns are bored with spiral rifling in order to give the projectile the spin necessary to keep it on target. And in football a forward pass must be thrown with a spiral if it is to stay on course and reach the receiver, free from wobbling or tumbling. Also a golf ball is maintained on the line by its numerous small dimples that give it stabilizing spin and lift, without which its flight would be highly erratic. Similarly, a tennis ball is hit with top spin, under spin, or side spin to obtain control of the length, height, and direction of its flight and type of bounce. Otherwise, it would be difficult to maneuver the ball with high speed and accuracy within a tennis court only 78 x 27 (singles) or 36 feet (doubles) in size. Further mention will be made of spin in later chapters.

Fortunately, the motions used in striking a tennis ball are similar to such natural movements as running, quick stops and starts, swinging a stick, and throwing a stone. While each of these requires some coordination and balance, the moves are so familiar that almost everyone can play the game.

The basic fundamentals of stroke production are composed of a sequence of essentially simple motions involving maintaining body balance as you move to meet the ball, and proper weight shift as you make your backswing, hit the ball, follow through, and return to the ready position.

Referring to the sequence of movements illustrated in Figure 5 will assist you in understanding the basic motions in making one standard

Figure 5: The Forehand Drive

stroke, the forehand drive. Also it will be helpful in picturing other portions of stroking techniques mentioned later.

Frame a shows the player in excellent ready or anticipatory position with racket pointed toward the net, knees bent slightly, and weight evenly distributed on the balls of the feet. In frame b the player is pushing off with his left foot and turning to the right to start his backswing with his left hand still on the racket, which importantly forces him to turn his shoulders. Frame c shows the body pivoting continuing with weight more on the right foot, racket backswing high, and left hand brought downward and sideward for balance. Frame d illustrates the ball approaching, with the player watching the ball intently with knees bent as he begins to turn his shoulders and shift his weight forward in preparation to striking the ball. Frame e shows the moment of hitting the ball slightly in front of the body with a closed stance (left foot nearer the sideline than the right foot) and racket face open to direct the ball down the sideline. (Note: This statement is worth dwelling on for a moment, as it is important to the art of anticipation. Were the striker trying to direct the ball cross court he would have a more open stance, with his left foot farther from the sideline than his right, and his racket would have to meet the ball farther in front of his body. Thus, the alert receiver should have anticipated the direction of the shot between frames d and e and begun moving to cover his backhand sideline.) Observe that the forearm, wrist, and racket are locked in a straight line to impart power to the shot. The footwork in this sequence is excellent. Without proper footwork to move into position with balance, you cannot strike the ball with regularity and accuracy. The final frame, f, shows the complete follow-through with racket head high to provide power. The weight is being redistributed back to both feet as the player watches the ball and his opponent and prepares to move to the ready position to await the anticipated next return. The entire stroke is so rhythmical that it appears effortless.

Three things characterize the play of all great tennis players. First, they make the game look relatively easy because they all utilize proper stroke-preparation methods. These entail sound footwork and fluid motions as they approach the ball with perfect balance and timing, resulting in economy of player motion and energy. Second, they all produce the various strokes within fairly narrow limits of orthodox style concepts at the vital moment of hitting the ball, although each player maintains a definite individuality matched to his physical makeup and prowess. In other words, certain basic principles of hitting the ball are utilized by all players, but there is no single perfect method of producing any particular tennis stroke. And, third, they have all practiced and studied their opposition so thoroughly that they invariably anticipate the opponent's shots and court position, and thus prepare for and make the best answering stroke despite the fact they usually have less than half a second to come to a decision.

While all of this makes fine reading, we wish to reiterate that the best method of learning the fundamentals and perfecting your stroking techniques is to take lessons from a competent teacher. Even the best players recognize it is difficult to perform self-diagnosis—a coach can spot and correct a flaw in your strokes far more easily and quickly.

4

THE SERVE

The serve is the single most important stroke in tennis for two major reasons. First, it is the most frequently used stroke in both singles (37.5 percent of all shots—see Table 6) and in doubles (30 percent, as shown in Table 7). Second, and more important, the serve puts the striker on the attack and thereby accounts directly or indirectly for from about 25 to 50 percent of all winning strokes in singles and doubles. This spread in effectiveness requires some explanation, as the velocity, placement, and spin of the serve and the type of court surface all influence the degree of lethality of the stroke.

SERVING BASICS IN SINGLES

Let us first consider the importance of the service in singles. Many ranking men can serve at speeds up to about 110 miles per hour, which means the ball will reach the receiver in just under half a second. On a fast court, such as used in most tournaments, the ball skids rapidly with a low bounce, so that the receiver can only move and reach about six to ten feet to his right or left to intercept the ball. To add further to the woes of the receiver, the spin on the ball can cause the bounce to change direction. All of this means the server can score a number of aces and forced errors. These, together with errors, will account for about 33 percent of all winning strokes (Table 6). But the true importance of the serve goes well beyond such numbers. The reasons for this are that the serve often draws a weak return or forces the receiver out of position, thus setting the stage for a winning first volley, or putting the receiver into a defensive predicament from which he cannot successfully extricate himself even after several exchanges. Therefore, in men's championship play on fast courts the serve is directly or indirectly responsible for winning about 50 percent of all points! Little question why we rank the serve as the most important stroke. For this reason, and because it requires precise coordination of ball toss, backswing, knee action, weight shift, foot movement, striking action, and follow-through, the serve should be practiced frequently and at length.

However, the game is much more complicated than that. If the court surface is slow, the effectiveness of the serve is reduced drastically, even if the speed remains the same. The reason is that the ball tends to dig into a slow composition or clay court, leaving a mark and bouncing slower and higher. This allows the receiver an additional small fraction of a second to cover more court, as well as to stand in closer to net to cut down the angle available for the service ball to spin to either side. These may appear to be unbelievably small changes. However, they combine to permit the wise receiver to cut down the level of outright service winners from about 33 to 23 percent (Table 6), and to blunt the ability of the server to gain the attacking area at net by his forward receiving position, from which point he can hit the higher-bounding ball aggressively down at the feet of a net-rushing server. In fact, by carrying out these tactics the receiver can reduce to very low numbers the points lost to first volleys (Table 6) and decrease the total points attributed directly or indirectly to the serve from about 50 percent to 25 percent.

The significance of the serve is also reduced in women's singles. Few women have the ability to serve at speeds exceeding 85 miles per hour, which means that the receiver has time to execute the return. The serve in women's singles is responsible directly or indirectly for from about 5 to 30 percent of all winning points, depending, once again, on court surface.

At this time it is appropriate to describe briefly the three basic service strokes. Most good players employ the Eastern backhand or Continental grip because these provide the wrist freedom to permit you to hit the nearly flat (no serve is totally without spin), slice, and twist serves with little change in ball toss and body motion. The grip is kept light to allow the wrist to remain supple in order to provide maximum wrist snap as the ball is struck. This all-important snap imparts both power and spin to the ball. The resulting serves are shown in Figure 6. The nearly flat serve is hit by directing the racket almost straight at the ball tossed directly overhead, the slice serve by directing the racket around, down, and over a ball tossed a bit farther to the right, and the twist serve by directing the racket up and over a ball tossed enough to the left so the back must arch as the stroke is produced. These small differences in ball tosses allow the discerning receiver to anticipate the type of serve about to be delivered.

Figure 6: The Three Basic Serves

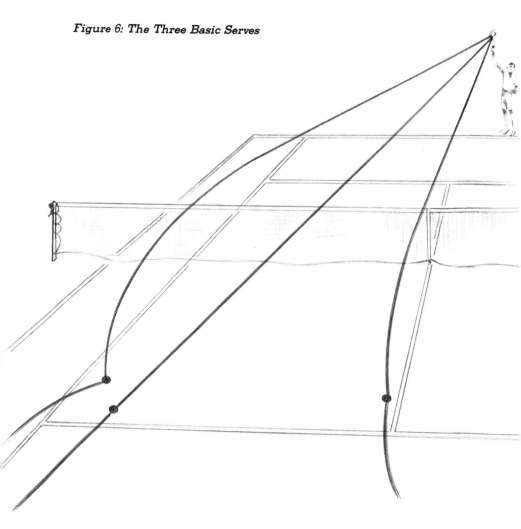

Since the server has two chances to produce a successful serve, the usual tactic is to take more risks with the first serve. It is hit flatter and harder, and the aim points are deeper or wider than for second serves (Figure 7). Therefore, it wins outright more points than the second serve (Table 6). This brings out the temptation, particularly in younger players, to overhit the ball and get far too few first serves into play. This is a very costly mistake, which we illustrate in Table 9. Data for both men and women show clearly that once you miss the first serve against a player of roughly equal ranking, the odds on winning the point become equal. On fast courts the higher-speed and deeper first serve results in the point being won ultimately three out of four times among the men and three out of five times for the slower-serving women. Therefore, it is ridiculous to blast your first serve out and waste all that energy, plus that of running partway to net, while at the same time reducing your chances of winning the point to even! The best servers often begin a match by easing up a bit on the first serve and putting more spin on the ball in order to hold it in the court. Once they get their rhythm and confidence established, they add to the speed. Top servers should get into play at least 70 percent of first serves. This is not easy—we have seen top professionals drop as low as 30 percent. The best first-service performance we ever measured was a fantastic 85 percent success rate in one championship professional match, which the server proceeded to win easily. Now you can better understand why we recommend practicing the serve!

TABLE 9

Effect of Serve on Outcome of Points in Singles

	FIRST SERVE		SECOND SERVE	
	Win	Lose	Win	Lose
FAST COURT				
Men	3	1	1	1
Women	1.5	1	1	1
SLOW COURT				
Men	2	1	1	1
Women	1.5	1	1	1

Figure 7

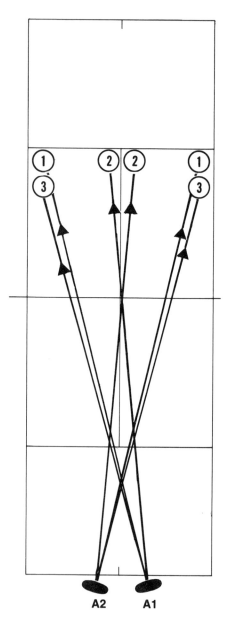

A2   A1

AIM POINTS FOR SERVES IN SINGLES

The preferred aim points for first serves are shown in Figure 7A. About 50 percent of serves to the forehand and backhand courts are aimed deep (within four feet of the service line) at area 1. The reason for this is that serves to the outside corner pull the receiver out of position wide of the court, thus opening up almost all of the cross-court area for a winning or forcing first volley or ground stroke. Some 30 percent of serves are hit to area 2·in the forehand court in order to take advantage of the weaker backhand side. Area 3 is used about 10 percent of the time for aiming sharply sliced serves to the forehand by righthanders and to the backhand court by lefthanders. About 30 percent of serves to the backhand court are aimed at area 2 to keep the receiver guessing. Further, the serve to the forehand down the middle does not give the receiver any opportunity for a wide-angle return.

Aim points for second serves (Figure 7B) are somewhat different in that areas 1 and 2 to the weaker backhand are the target of about 75 percent of all serves. This is made easier because the safe, high American twist serve is naturally directed there. Slices to area 3 are for surprise, and to keep the receiver from running around his backhand. Note that the aim points are more shallow than for first serves in order to avoid double faults. Serves landing even shorter, near the middle of the service court, must be shunned, as they give the offense away to the receiver.

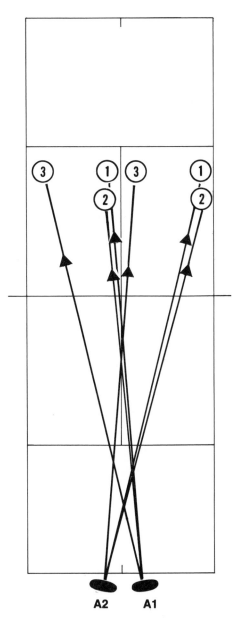

SERVING TACTICS IN SINGLES

Fast-Court Play

The serve has three major objectives: (1) to put the ball into play in a manner aimed at gaining the offense by forcing the receiver into making a weak return or moving out of position, (2) to follow in behind serve to the attacking net position, and (3) to study the receiver while running to the net position in order to anticipate the type, speed, and direction of the return of service.

In order to achieve these objectives, it is first necessary to place the serve properly. The aim-point priorities are shown in Figure 7, along with pertinent comments. Some further information will be helpful to the reader in grasping the significance of the serve, such as:

- Deep first serves, landing within about four feet of the service line, ultimately win points approximately 75 percent of the time. Clearly, this makes the big serve a must for top-flight singles play today.
- Deep first serves provide the striker a better chance to put away a winning first volley by a three-to-two ratio over second serves.
- The key factor in the second serve is also depth. The balance between winning or losing the majority of second serves hangs delicately on the matter of depth. You can win about 50 percent of second serves provided the serve is deep.

So much for the placement of the serve in connection with carrying out the first objective of the server—that of gaining the offense. The second and third objectives call for getting into the net position and thinking and anticipating while so doing. On a fast court the modern game calls for following in behind every serve to the net position, with important exceptions to be mentioned in a moment. The proper path to the net varies with the type and placement of the serve and the anticipated return of service. Examples of this will be explored more thoroughly under net play. At this moment it suffices to say that you should swing your foot over the base line as you hit the service and sprint for the net. While doing so, you must concentrate your attention not on the ball but on the receiver in order to anticipate the type, direction, and speed of the return of service.

Having just recommended capturing the attacking position by following serve into net, we must note that not all top tennis players utilize these "big game" tactics. In fact, some recent world's champions in both the men's and women's divisions have won by employing a powerful base-line game with passing shots sufficiently deadly to blunt the opponent's net play, even on fast courts. But then there inevitably appears on the horizon a player cast in the serve-and-volley mold who will oust the base-liner from the pinnacle. That, of course, is what makes tennis such a great game—its variety is endless and there is no absolutely correct way to execute tactics. Instead, each player must adapt the basics to maximize his own capabilities.

Slow-Court Play

Data on slow-court play were collected at the U.S. National Clay Court Championship and during matches played on composition courts. The slow-court game is entirely different, as the strokes responsible for winners attest (see Table 6). This is why some of the big hitters are missing from the lists of the French Championship titleholders, as the notoriously slow courts used tilt the advantage to the steady ground-stroke artist with stamina.

Unlike fast-court play, not even the very best servers can serve and volley consistently on a slow court against an opponent with respectable return-of-service skills. As noted in Table 6, only a paltry 2 percent of all winning shots in slow-court play are made with first volleys. Therefore, we recommend that following the first serve in to net should be restricted to two situations: (1) to inject an element of surprise so that the receiver is kept under constant pressure to note whether you are coming in, while also watching the ball, and (2) to prevent the receiver from hitting safe high returns—after you volley away a few, the opponent will have to resort to riskier lower returns. A second recommendation is that the server avoid completely trying to take the net on a second serve.

The aim points for placing the first and second serves on slow-courts are the same as for fast courts, with one exception. In serving to the forehand court most players prefer to place the first serve into the backhand instead of the forehand corner (see Figure 7) about 50 percent of the time and to use other parts of the court as surprise variants. The reason, of course, is that you are no longer trying to open up the court for an easy first volley.

The two most important tactics to remember have to do with preventing the receiver from stealing away the offensive. The first entails

Figure 8

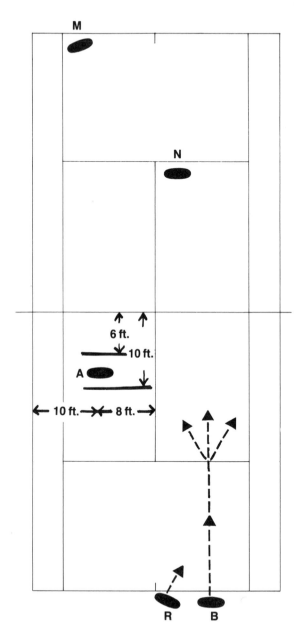

SERVING AND RECEIVING TEAM POSITIONS IN DOUBLES

Server B stands midway between the center of the base line and the sideline, leaving him the shortest route to the proper net position and a better chance to change direction to intercept the return of service than if he had started from R, the normal serving position in singles. The server's partner A stands from six to ten feet from the net (depending on his height and agility in covering lobs, and whether the opponents are using the lob), and about one or two feet toward the center beyond the midpoint between sideline and center line. There are two reasons why the net man should crowd the center. First, since most returns of service are cross court, crowding the center permits the net man to volley easily any errant down-the-middle returns. And, second, it provides him with a head-start position for "poaching" rapidly with surprise to volley away for winners seemingly effective cross-court returns of service. More about "poaching" a bit later.

The receiving-team standard formation has receiver M just inside the base line and net man N in the modified net position.

getting the first serve in as often as possible, even if this means hitting the ball at about three-quarters speed. The second point is to try to hit both first and second serves deep. These tactics are both aimed at preventing the receiver from risking moving forward on the serve so that he can make a forcing return and assume the offensive. In actual practice, deep serves result in the server winning points at a comfortable two-to-one ratio, whereas shallow serves result in a struggle to achieve a one-to-one standoff. The reasons for this will become clear in Chapter 4 on "Return of Service."

SERVING BASICS IN DOUBLES

The service stroke in doubles is, if anything, even more important than the serve in singles. In good doubles play a loss of serve is the cardinal sin, as most sets are decided by but a single break in service.

There is strong evidence to back up the importance of the serve. We have already seen in Chapter 2 that doubles is won by taking and maintaining the offensive position, which is at the net. The successful serve in doubles has two major objectives: First, it attempts to win the point by forcing the receiver into an error or weak return, and, second, it is supposed to provide the server a safe journey in to the attacking position at net at the start of each point. Furthermore, as noted in Chapter 2 (Table 7), this important starting stroke is the one most frequently used in doubles.

In this chapter the play of the serving team will be taken only as far as preparing for the volley of the return of service. The play from that point on will be discussed in Chapter 5, on "Net Play."

The proper normal positions for serving-team players A and B in either the forehand or backhand court are shown in Figure 8. There are also some unconventional serving formations which will be mentioned later. Receiving team members M and N will be discussed in Chapter 4.

To carry out the two aforementioned primary objectives of the server, he must employ the weapons of speed, spin, and placement of the service. All outstanding doubles players agree that the one most important objective in serving is to put the *first service* into play. The logical reasons for this are several. First, the receiver must position himself deeper in fear that a fast first service may produce an ace or force a weak, losing return. Second, the fact that the receiver is positioned deeper permits the server to gain a step or two in his tactic of dashing

Figure 9

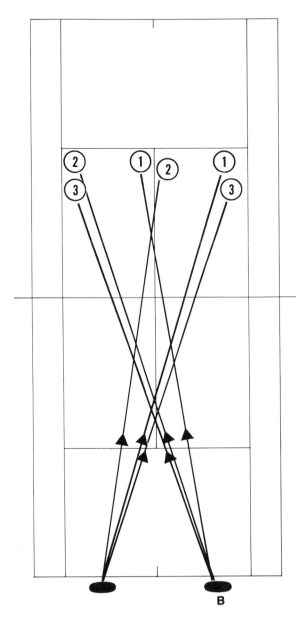

B

AIM POINTS FOR SERVES IN DOUBLES

The preferred aim points for first serves in doubles are shown in this diagram. About 80 percent of first serves are hit to area 1 on the opponent's weaker backhand side in both courts. These are usually twist or spin serves hit safely high over the net at about three-fourths speed in order to get the first serve into play because of the great tactical advantage it provides. The slice serve to area 2 or 3 is usually employed as a surprise variant to keep the receiver from running around his backhand. The slice is also useful in serving to the backhand of a lefty. The nearly flat cannonball serve is not a good gamble in doubles, as it often misses, and also cuts down on the time available to the server in running to the offensive position at net.

The aim points for the second serve are the same as for the first serve, but the aim points are slightly more shallow in order to avoid double faults. The spot to avoid is a shallow serve to the middle, which gives the receiver the opportunity to move in and take the offensive (see Figure 12).

toward the all-important net position. And, third, a combination of items one and two results in a vanishing capability of the receiver to take away the offensive by moving forward in order to return service down and low at the vulnerable feet of the net-rushing server. More about such receiving tactics in Chapter 4.

The benefits of this advice become crystal clear as we now examine data on the advantages of getting the first service into play over the second service. The serving team ultimately wins from 70 to 80 percent of all points when the first serve is good. When the first serve is a fault, the receiver can move forward to hit the weaker second serve from a better attacking position. Data show the receiver can follow his return into the offensive position at net six times as often on successful returns of the second service as on successful returns of first service. This has a devastating effect, as the serving team ultimately wins only from 30 to 50 percent of points on second serves. An added danger is that missed second serves result in double faults, and no player has ever won a point that way. Remember, even the best servers in tennis avoid blasting the first serve in doubles in order to seek the tactical advantage of getting the first ball safely into play. Take heed, and concentrate on developing a reliable first serve, and a controlled second serve of only slightly less speed.

The preferred aim points for first and second serves in doubles are shown in Figure 9. At this time a preliminary explanation of the reasoning behind these recommended aim points should assist the reader in understanding the important tactical considerations.

At the outset it must be recognized that the act of serving in doubles requires teamwork, with each player having important duties.

The server's duties can be summarized as follows:

• Upon striking the ball he must bring his trailing foot over the base line and sprint for the net in a straight line, taking a series of long steps. (This run for the net must take place on every serve until a fault is obvious or called, as stopping and being caught halfway can lose the point.) Following about four long steps, the server should bring both feet together with weight equally distributed at a point just short of the service line so that he is prepared to hop and then move in any direction. At that moment he must anticipate the most likely type of return of service, depending on the bounce point of the serve and his study of the stroking actions of the receiver. Then he must move toward the proper area to intercept the ball as close to the net as possible (the importance of this will be covered in Chapter 5), or to reverse and retrieve lobs. The server should also familiarize himself with the latest foot-fault rules. On one hand, it is unfair to take advantage of opponents by getting an important head start toward the net position. On the other hand, it can be very discouraging to serve an apparent winner at a vital moment in an important match and have it ruled a foot fault.

The net man also has several duties in order to assist in gaining or maintaining the offensive for the serving team, as follows:

• The net man must watch the served ball move past him and determine its speed, spin, and where it will land in the service court. A split second later he should shift his attention from the ball to the receiver in order to try to anticipate from the ball position and the receiver's stance, backswing, and the manner in which he prepares to produce his stroke what type of shot will result—flat or topped drive, angled spin or dink, or lob—and in what direction. Continued study of any receiver should increase the net man's ability to anticipate more accurately. The net man is now ready to reposition himself to give the serving team the optimum offensive formation. If he anticipates a return down the sideline, to the middle, or sharply cross court, he should move to the left or right to cover his portion of court-area responsibility. If he foresees a lob, the net man should retreat a step or two and be prepared to try to play the ball with his stronger forehand overhead. A very important, if not the most vital, factor in net-man play is the matter of timing. No move, other than a fake, should be made before the receiver is fully committed to make his shot. The interval of time between the anticipation and the move is extremely brief. A premature start is likely to leave an opening for a placement behind the net man's move. The skilled player waits until that brief instant between when the receiver is sufficiently committed so as not to be able to alter his stroke, and the moment when the ball is struck. That is precisely when the net man can poach cross court to win points (more on poaching later). As one expert player stated: "Half the art of anticipation is to conceal the fact that you have anticipated."

Continued concentration by the net man should enable him to guess the enemy plans and win or save many points in each set. And mental lapses and ill-timed moves can embarrass your partner, and lose points as well.

It is now timely to examine in some detail the tactical implications and effects of three different service aim points.

First, reference should be made to Figure 10, which explains the advantages accruing to the serving team from directing the first serve to aim point 1, the backhand corner of the forehand court. Remember that we are in every instance considering a *team effort* in describing the movements of the serving duo.

Second, the reasons why aim point 2 produces less advantageous offensive positions for the serving team are well illustrated in Figure 11. The slice serve to the forehand court opens up wide angles for the return from the stronger forehand side. That is why this serve is used only sparingly to keep the receiver honest. A slice serve to area 2 in the backhand court is not as risky, since the receiver has only narrow angles open from the center of the base line for his trusted forehand return. The wide serve to the backhand corner of the backhand court does not present the severe angle problems of the forehand court, since the return has to be played from the normally weaker backhand side. Trying to run around such a serve to play it from the forehand would force the receiver way out of court.

And, third, the great disadvantage created by the short serve is graphically illustrated in Figure 12.

The tactics for serving are the same for women's and men's doubles. If for some reason you are not able to follow your serve in to net, the rule should be to get there on the very first shot you can, because doubles is won at the net.

The service is a duel between the server and the receiver, with each trying to gain an advantage so that the second shot by his team can be an offensive one. This means the server must continually study the receiver, his position, stroke techniques, movements, return habits, and try to outguess him through anticipation. The odds favor the server because he begins with the offense. He must push this advantage to the utmost.

Unconventional Serving Formations

Two axioms of the sporting world—keep the opponents off balance and change tactics if losing—are responsible for the birth of the unconventional stratagem in every game. It is only logical that surprise changes of serving formations should become important elements in the game of doubles.

Near the turn of the century both the Americans and the Australians

Figure 10

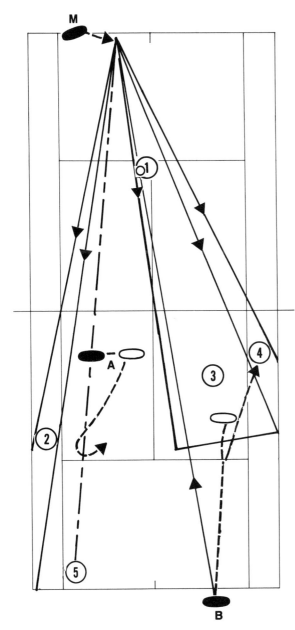

EFFECT OF PLACEMENT OF SERVE ON POSSIBLE ANGLES OF RETURN OF SERVICE

A deep serve to the preferred aim point, area 1, is the strongest gambit because it gives the serving team the safest journey to gain the all-important net position.

A return by receiver M to area 2 is unlikely, since great accuracy is required to hit that narrow angle over the high portion of the net. This permits net man A to simplify the server's job. On seeing the serve bounce in area 1 and noting the receiver commit himself to the more logical cross-court return, net man A can slide over, as shown, to cover the center of the court. This permits server B to note this move and come up a bit wider to cover backhands or runaround forehands hit to area 3, and sharply angled shots directed to area 4. The latter must be hit softly over the higher net at the sideline in order to stay in the court, thus giving the server added time to swerve and intercept them. Lobs hit by receiver M from the center of the court to area 5 can be handled effectively by net man A, who can usually drop back and play them on his stronger forehand overhead side.

Figure 11

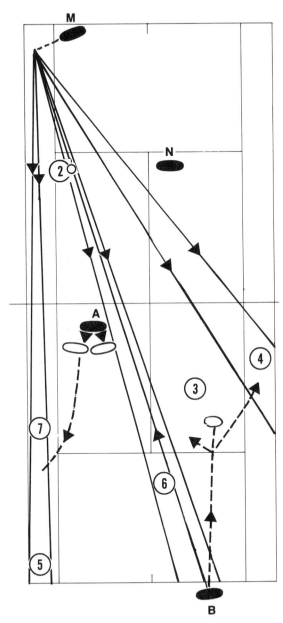

EFFECT OF PLACEMENT OF SERVE ON POSSIBLE ANGLES OF RETURN OF SERVICE

A slice serve to aim ·point 2 is recommended as a surprise ploy from time to time to throw the receiver off balance in hopes of drawing a weak return. However, if receiver M is alert and in position, the serving team faces a difficult task defending against a strong forehand in combination with wider available return angles.

Net man A faces a tough choice. If he makes the preferred move to his left to cover a drive down the alley to area 7, or a lob hit to his weak backhand overhead to area 5, he leaves the center area 6 open. Conversely, if he moves to the right to cover the center, as he did in Figure 10, he leaves the alley unguarded. The server must observe the moves of the receiver and of his net man and choose between covering the center areas 6 and 3 or the wide shot to area 4. This latter area is particularly difficult to defend because, unlike the slow, soft dink shown in Figure 10, the receiver can hit a severe topped cross-court forehand drive over the lower portion of the net and keep it in court.

Obviously, on serves to aim point 2 the serving team must anticipate the return and set up their offensive positions unerringly, or the opponents can hit through a hole for a placement or forced error.

Figure 12

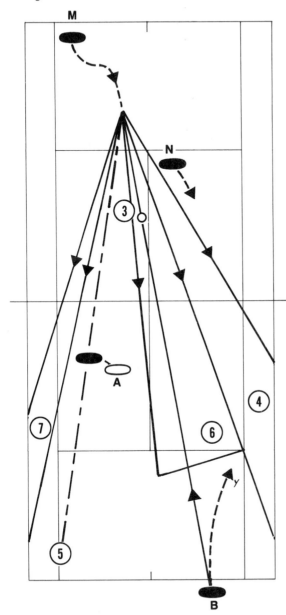

THE HAZARDS OF THE SHALLOW SERVE

A shallow serve is likely to bring on disaster in that it often hands the offense over to the receiving team.

Receiver M, as indicated, can move in and run around a serve hit to area 3 in order to play the ball with his strong forehand. From close in he has his choice of hitting to open spots at area 7, 6, or 4, or lobbing to area 5, depending on the positions of the serving team. Their positions are hardly enviable, as net man A has little time to move under point-blank range from receiver M, and server B does not have time to approach closer to the net than position Y. This means that receiver M has the opportunity to glance at the positions of the serving team and play forcing shots to area 7 or 4, drives to the vulnerable position at the feet of server B in area 6, or lobs over the head of net man A to area 5.

The outcome of shallow serves would be expected to be disastrous, and it is. Serving teams lose over 50 percent of such points.

experimented with a reverse formation for the serving team. The practice of placing the net man on the same side of the court as the server (shown in Figure 13A) was designed to offset an outstanding cross-court return of service. In other words, the server just got very tired of digging beautifully placed returns of service out of the turf and losing many points as a result of his weak first volleys. Instead of despairing, the inventor decided to change tactics and try a new formation. There are two reasons why this made good sense. First, the net man can take up the best defensive position against the return of service, and not be forced to move very far to make the volley. Second, the receiver, faced with an offsetting defense for his practiced return, is usually less effective whenever he elects to play down the line at the server coming up the reverse side.

Properly executed, unconventional serving formations can be most disconcerting to the opponents. With the variety of formations, poaches, and fakes used against him, the receiver can literally be driven to distraction. The receiver is forced by such tactics to watch the movements of the serving team, as well as the ball, until the last split second, so that he is more likely to err. In important tournaments several teams are likely to use well-practiced unconventional formations to advantage. In general, the plays are triggered by signals set up before the point as the net man turns his back to the net and faces the server. Variety in play is the keynote. Figure 13 shows some of the permutations and combinations. Note that several fake plays are possible from each formation.

Unconventional formations and fakes require the partners to practice signals and timing. Nothing makes a team feel more foolish than to pull a tricky maneuver and have it backfire. For example, one of the authors played a match in the late afternoon against a team which had this poaching maneuver: the server came up the reverse side whenever the net man signaled a poach by scratching his back. This particular evening the gnats were not only out in force but biting savagely. Unfortunately, the net man often forgot himself and scratched vigorously at frequent intervals. This was so confusing to the server that in the first set many points were lost as one whole side of the court was left unguarded. Happily, the humor of the situation saved the scratching team, and it went on to win.

Figure 13

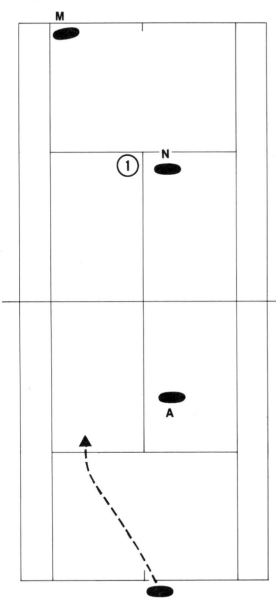

UNCONVENTIONAL SERVING FORMATIONS IN DOUBLES

Figure 13A shows the reverse formation with the serving team having both players on the same side of the court. This is used sometimes to try to upset a receiver who has an outstanding cross-court return by placing net man A in the best position to volley the return from a serve hit to aim point 1.

Figure 13B depicts the surprise and the signaled poaches. On the surprise poach, server B follows his normal path to the net until he sees the poach and then veers to his left along path 2 to cover the open court. On the signaled poach, server B aims his serve to area 1 and follows his normal path toward the net for a couple of steps, so as not to reveal the poach, and then runs left along path 3.

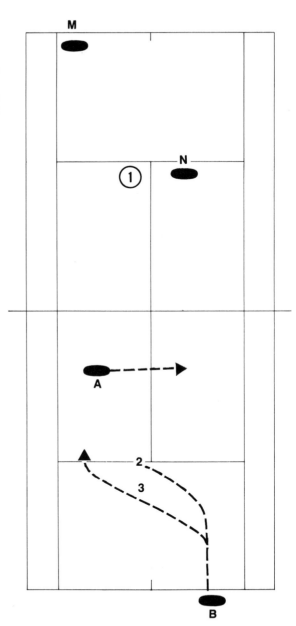

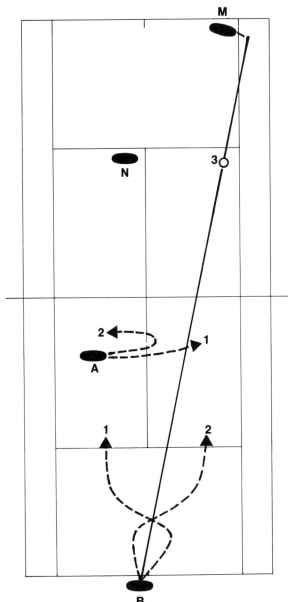

Figure 13C illustrates two fakes from the reverse serving formation. In case 1 server B runs in as though he were going to cover the open side until receiver M is committed, at which moment net man A poaches and B swerves to his left. In case 2 net man A fakes the poach and B moves in to his left a bit before changing ˙direction when receiver M is drawn into playing a cross-court return.

Figure 13D shows two fakes from the conventional serving formation. In case 1 the net man fakes a poach and server B carries out the fake by going to his left. If successful in drawing the down-the-line return, net man A should have an easy volley for the point. In case 2 net man A fakes left to cover the alley after a slice serve to draw a cross-court return before executing the poach. Server B carries out his role by faking straight in before swerving left.

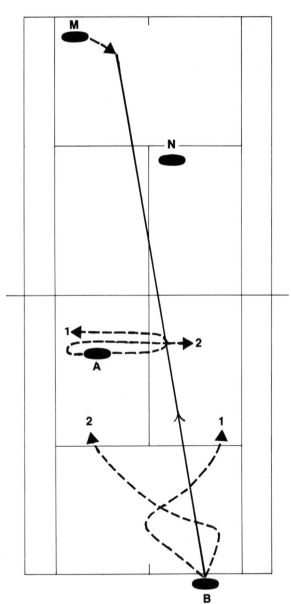

5

RETURN OF SERVICE

A sound return of service is vital to greatness in both singles and doubles. Without doubt, it is one of the most difficult strokes in tennis to execute both effectively and consistently. This is demonstrated by the fact that 20 to 25 percent of serves in singles and doubles are not returned at all, service is broken only about once in five to seven games, and the stroke has a low potency (see Table 8).

The receiver must remember that no one ever won a set without breaking the opponent's serve at least once. And, of course, you cannot win a point by failing to return service (other than by means of a double fault). Therefore, the main duty of the receiver is to get the ball back by any possible means—even the worst return sometimes wins a point. And the player who can develop a reliable return will own an invaluable asset. If he can then add control and disguise to his stroke, he advances to the exalted company of the world-class players.

The tactics for returns of service differ substantially between singles and doubles, and we shall now explore each separately.

RECEIVING IN SINGLES

The receiver should have in mind the following five objectives:

- Adopt the most advantageous receiving position to assert your strength, your best return.
- Anticipate the type of serve to be delivered.

- Return the ball at all costs.
- Force the server into making a defensive return.
- Capture the net at the earliest opportunity.

The proper position for the receiver can be determined by simple logic. If you master the factors which govern good position play, you will win a lot of points as a receiver. Since some players never seem to develop such an understanding, let us proceed to diagram these in order to explain them clearly. Figure 14 illustrates the basic receiver positions corresponding to differing server positions.

However, these basic receiving positions have to be altered under certain circumstances. The receiver must learn *to anticipate the type of serve* and to reposition himself accordingly—inches make a difference in receiving success. Over the years there has been a trend toward moving inside the base line as far as one dares in order to try to counter the serve-and-volley or "big" game. There are three reasons why this makes tactical sense: (1) The earlier you return service, the less time the server has to reach the proper volleying position. (2) The earlier you hit the ball, the easier it is to cover court, as the speed and spin of the serve have less opportunity to pull you wide of the court. (3) The closer you are to the service line, the easier it is, particularly on second serves, to take the net away from the server. The great importance of anticipating the second serve, moving forward, hitting an offensive return, and taking net is attested to by the fact that this tactic has decided many important women's and men's championships over the past fifty years. While a few top-ranking players have been able to win staying on the base line, most grab every opportunity to steal away the net.

Anticipation is an art which requires keen observation. Every server has a particular set of characteristics which, if studied, should permit the receiver to diagnose the type of delivery. Most servers telegraph the shot by the way they toss the ball. For example, many players toss a bit to the right and in front for a slice serve, and swing across the body; toss straight up and in front for a flat serve; and toss a bit to the left and swing up and over along the base line to hit an American twist serve. Some have favorite aim points for certain point-score situations. Others may be enticed into hitting a particular serve by the receiving position you take. And still others have small stroke-production characteristics which give away intentions. Also you may have certain receiving weaknesses of which the server is aware, so that you can expect to be bombarded with shots aimed at taking advantage of these. It is hardly possi-

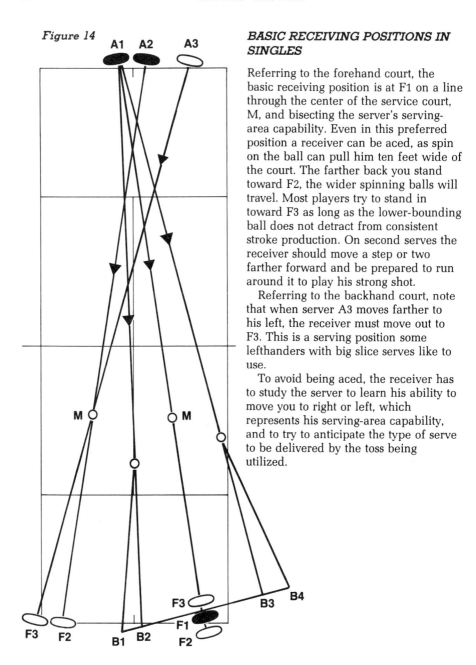

Figure 14

BASIC RECEIVING POSITIONS IN SINGLES

Referring to the forehand court, the basic receiving position is at F1 on a line through the center of the service court, M, and bisecting the server's serving-area capability. Even in this preferred position a receiver can be aced, as spin on the ball can pull him ten feet wide of the court. The farther back you stand toward F2, the wider spinning balls will travel. Most players try to stand in toward F3 as long as the lower-bounding ball does not detract from consistent stroke production. On second serves the receiver should move a step or two farther forward and be prepared to run around it to play his strong shot.

Referring to the backhand court, note that when server A3 moves farther to his left, the receiver must move out to F3. This is a serving position some lefthanders with big slice serves like to use.

To avoid being aced, the receiver has to study the server to learn his ability to move you to right or left, which represents his serving-area capability, and to try to anticipate the type of serve to be delivered by the toss being utilized.

ble to overemphasize the value of keen anticipation in helping the receiver overcome the many difficulties he faces in his duel against the competent server. On top of this, the receiver must practice his balance, ability to make quick starts in any direction, take the ball on the rise, make his return, and move immediately to the correct position for the next shot.

The receiver's third and most basic objective is *to get the ball back* in any way possible. Beginner and experienced player alike must work on achieving success in this department. After all, you cannot win the point if you do not keep the ball in play, and often even the feeblest, saddest return will draw an error from a greedy or over-anxious opponent. By returning in some way everything thrown at you, even with high defensive lobs, you exert relentless pressure upon the server. Many servers become unsettled when they have to win every point the hard way rather than from errors, and this leads to service breaks.

There is one fact about return of service that should be engraved indelibly on the mind of the receiver. Data collected on hundreds of points in many matches clearly demonstrate that the receiver has almost an even chance of winning a given point providing he or she has successfully returned service. So it pays off handsomely to anticipate the type of serve, move quickly to reach the proper position, watch the ball, and develop a consistent return. To give you a comparative measure so you can rate your performance, top players return about seven out of ten serves on fast courts. On slow courts they return close to eight out of ten because of the higher bounce and the fact they can play a safer return, higher and deeper, since the server is much less likely to take the net. Some of the ranking women playing against less severe serves have even better return performances.

Now it is time to turn our attention to the fourth objective of the receiver: *to force the server into making a defensive shot* so that the receiver can take command. The techniques to accomplish this will have to be considered in two parts: the shots to make, first, when the server rushes the net, and, second, when the server remains on the base line.

Return of Service When Server Rushes the Net

There are two major points to keep in mind in returning serve against the player who follows serve in to net. These are (1) to take the ball as early as possible and keep the return low so that the server will not have time to get on top of the net and will be forced to volley up defen-

Figure 15

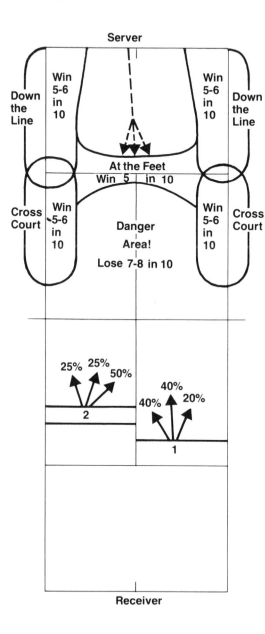

COMPOSITE PICTURE OF RETURNS OF SERVICE IN SINGLES AGAINST THE NET-RUSHING SERVER

The bottom portion of this diagram indicates on the forehand side that about 40 percent of returns from deep serves to area 1 are hit cross court, 40 percent to the middle, and 20 percent down the line. On the backhand side it indicates that returns from shallow serves hit to area 2 are returned 50 percent cross court, 25 percent to the middle, and 25 percent down the line.

The top part of the diagram indicates the reason why the receivers are attempting to avoid returns to the middle. Those hit at the approaching volleyer in the Danger Area result in losing points about seven to eight out of ten times. On the other hand, balls successfully aimed either cross court or down the line cause the volleyer to stretch out of position, and the receiver should ultimately win the point 55 to 60 percent of the time. Returns landing in the At the Feet area win about half the time.

The types of strokes employed in making these shots are low drives or spinning shots, or strokes utilizing top spin, in order to force the server to volley up.

sively, and (2) to keep the server guessing by mixing up cross-court and down-the-line drives, dinks, and occasional lobs. Avoid hitting to the middle.

The aim points used by the expert for return of service against the net rusher vary with the location from which the shot must be played. A great deal of information was collected on this subject during many tournament matches—on both grass and clay courts—involving the top players of the world. To provide some guidelines, let us take a look at a composite picture of the good and bad return aim points as presented in Figure 15.

Return of Service When Server Remains on the Base Line

Only a limited number of players in the world have a sufficiently powerful service to permit them to play the big game and follow every serve in to net. And even the international experts can ill afford to do so when playing on slow courts. Therefore, the great majority of readers will ordinarily return service against an opponent standing near the middle of the base line. This calls for completely different tactics from those just described. Instead of playing low drive or spinning angled returns which force the net-rushing server to hit up weak volleys, the whole purpose now is to hit deep returns to keep the server pinned to his defensive position on the base line. They should be hit one or more feet safely above the net to avoid costly netting errors—a common mistake of the weekend player. The strokes can be flat or top-spin or sliced drives, chops or even high, soft shots (half lobs)—anything which lands within ten feet of the base line. The objective is to make the return also sufficiently forcing so that the receiver can take the attacking position at net. On shallow serves in particular, the receiver must try to hit deep to the aim points shown in Figure 16 and rush the net. Weekend players in particular prefer returning deep to the backhand side. And, to drive home the importance of directing the return to the proper area, note how the chances of ultimately winning the point change.

Since the recommended return tactics change abruptly, depending upon the decision of the server to remain on the base line or to rush the net, the first duty of the receiver after anticipating the type and direction of serve is to note whether the server is rushing the net or staying on the base line. This fact controls the type of return to be employed. If, for example, you play an excellent high, deep shot toward the base line only to find too late that the server has elected to rush the net, you have

Figure 16

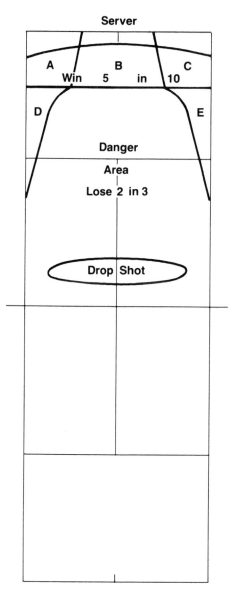

Server

A
B
C
Win   5   in   10

D   E

Danger

Area

Lose 2 in 3

Drop Shot

COMPOSITE PICTURE OF RETURNS OF SERVICE IN SINGLES AGAINST A SERVER REMAINING ON THE BASE LINE

In contrast to the low, spinning shots recommended for play against the net-rushing server, high, deep shots are best against the server who stays back.

The primary objective should be to keep the ball deep to area A, B, or C—that is, within ten feet of the base line. If you just do that, you should win half the points. Aiming for the deepest area shown is risky. Hitting to the corner at A or C helps by running the server. On shallow serves, sharply angled cross-court shots to area D or E sometimes win points outright or set up the win by forcing the server wide of the court. Drop shots should be employed only after shallow serves against an opponent who does not cover court speedily.

Returns to the Danger Area are to be avoided, as the receiver loses about two out of three times.

presented him with an easy volley for a win. Or if you played a low, angled return trying to embarrass the net-rushing server only to discover he has stayed back, you end up by awarding him an easy trip to the net.

RECEIVING IN DOUBLES

Ranking close to the serve as the most important shot in doubles is the return of service—after all, you have to break the opponent's serve at least once in order to win a set. Wherever it ranks in importance, the service return certainly ranks first in the minds of the experts in degree of difficulty to play both consistently and effectively. As evidence, service is seldom broken in good doubles more than once a set. And this is largely the responsibility of the receiver, because it is the quality of his return of service that determines the tactics of both teams at the start of each point.

The receiver faces a terrible predicament, as one half of the court is already covered by the net man, and the server is fast approaching the net to patrol the other half. This means that in the split-second period when he has to make his decision on the type and direction of his return, he must keep an eye on the net man to determine whether he will poach, an eye on the server to note his positioning, and an eye on the ball in order to be able to stroke it properly. That is not easy when you have only two eyes! Nevertheless, some of the great playmakers in doubles managed to return as many as nine out of ten serves.

The receiver in doubles should have the same five objectives as the receiver in singles:

- Adopt the most advantageous receiving position.
- Anticipate the type and direction of serve.
- Return the ball at all costs—do not forget the defensive lob.
- Force the serving team into making a defensive return.
- Capture the net at the earliest opportunity.

The *proper receiving positions* for the receiving team are shown in Figure 8. The receiver is close to the basic receiving position used in singles. Better yet, he should move forward a bit, as the server in doubles must elect to get his first ball into play rather than to chance going for an ace. The partner of the receiver should assume the modified net position just inside the service line near the center of the court. The

Figure 17

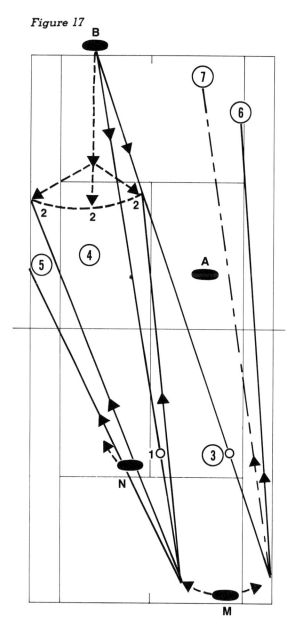

RETURNS OF DEEP SERVES IN DOUBLES

The returns of deep serves to the middle to point 1 in doubles are almost always directed cross court to unoccupied area 4, which represents the safest return territory. A few returns can be hit wide and offensively with dinks to area 5 to force the server to volley up.

Returns of deep serves wide to point 3 are also usually returned cross court to area 4. However, the possibility opens up for a drive down the line to aim point 6 if net man A is not alert. And if the serve forces you to play a defensive shot, a high lob to area 7 can be very effective. If hit about forty feet high and deep, it gives you and your partner time to call out instructions to one another to align defensive positions.

purpose of this formation, invented by the famous Doherty brothers in England in 1903, is to permit the receiving team to take advantage of a good return by moving rapidly in to the net position. The advantages of this formation are dependent upon effective returns of service, as will be shown later. If player N positions himself on the base line instead, the serving team is presented with an easier first volley and control of the net. And the net is the place doubles matches are won.

Anticipating the type and direction of serve is easier in doubles than in singles. As already discussed in chapter 3, the first serve in doubles is usually hit with spin at about three-fourths speed to obtain control and consistency, because the second serve is vulnerable to successful attack by the receiver. Furthermore, the preponderance of serves are aimed at the backhand corner in both courts. The receiver's main anticipation duties are thus reduced to avoiding being surprised by occasional fast or change-of-direction serves, to moving as far forward as possible in playing the return, and to "roll" with the serve by anticipating serves which you can run around to play from your stronger side.

The wisdom of returning the ball at all costs is evident when it is recognized that almost half the points won after a return is hit over the net are on errors by the serving team. Many a "sitter" has been hit out by the best of players.

We now approach the most important subject of the types of shots to force the serving team into making a defensive return. We will examine several ways of accomplishing this. The first principle is to hit the ball to an unoccupied area. As can be seen in Figure 17, the most obvious open spot is area 4, which requires a cross-court return of service. In fact, at least 80 percent of doubles returns of service are cross court to try to force the server into a weak return or an error. The second principle is to keep the return low. A high ball can be volleyed down offensively and devastatingly by server B or net man A. Hitting soft, high, floater returns can endanger not only the valued friendship of your modified-net-man partner, but also his very life as he tries to dodge bullets. In order to keep the ball low, a variety of types of strokes can be employed, such as the drive, top-spin drive, and dink just as used in singles against the net-rushing server. The third principle is to hit the ball on the rise as far forward as you dare. The reasons for this are that the sooner you strike the ball, the less spin to move you to the side, the less time available to the server to run to points 2 in Figure 17, the better position you have to direct the ball downward at the feet of the server or at sharper angles to the sidelines, and the quicker you can take the net position as you enjoy a head start. And *capturing the net at the earliest possible opportunity* is the fourth and final objective of the receiver, because he desires to take the offensive away from the serving team.

We are now ready to turn our attention to aim points on returns of service, beginning with deep serves to the forehand court, as shown in Figure 17. The predominance and effectiveness of the cross-court return of service arise in part from a purely mechanical basis. The net in tennis is six inches lower at the center than at the sideline, so that it is obviously easier to direct a lower return cross court over the middle portion of the net from deep in the backhand or forehand corner of the court. This helps to force the server to volley the ball up from his shoe tops with less severity. And the down-the-line return to area 7 is necessarily a higher return over the highest part of the net. This means net man A can deal with it offensively by hitting down on the ball unless you catch him by surprise or out of position. Receiver M must study the tactics of the server and mix up his returns accordingly. If the server has trouble with trying to reach and volley the spinning, low dink or slice shots hit to area 5, he may slow down and play the ball after the bounce. This calls for a change in tactics to hitting top-spin or low, flat drives at the feet of the server to pin him deep in the service court.

The type of return chosen by the receiver naturally depends in part on his own stroke repertoire as well as the playing abilities of the opponents. Some of the reasoning behind stroke choice for returns will become clearer when we proceed into actual complete-point play in Chapters 5 and 6. A few remarks here on the attributes of the various strokes may be helpful.

The dink, or soft chop or slice shot, has been the favorite service return of many of the greatest women and men doubles players. It is usually played sharply cross court out of reach of the net man. There are three reasons why it is favored. First, it is a safe shot which enables the receiver to put the ball into play consistently. Second, it is so soft that it prevents the receiver from getting much pace on his volley, which must be hit up in most cases. And, third, its slow velocity allows the modified net man and the receiver time to get in to net to gain the opportunity of stealing the offense away from the serving team. One drawback to the dink is that it is difficult to play off the occasional deep, flat, cannonball service.

The next favored return of service is a top-spin cross-court drive, also used by many great doubles players. It has many of the advantages of the dink in that it is safe, since it can be hit well above net, and it forces the server to volley up, as it dips low after crossing the net. Since the top-spin drive is hit harder than the dink, it is volleyed back with more pace, giving the receiver and the modified net man less time to run into the net.

Against a fast service many experts prefer a rather flat cross-court drive. Its principal advantage is that a fast, hard return will often draw an error, as it forces the server to volley up from deep in the court. As a standard return, it is difficult to play consistently and it leaves the receiver little possibility to follow it in to net. The drive is also played down the line from time to time as a check shot designed to keep the net man "honest," by preventing him from promiscuous poaching.

The fourth type of stroke for return of service is the lob. Use of the offensive lob is described in Figure 18, which depicts aim points for returns on shallow serves. It is also effective if you catch the net man crowding the net or moving prematurely. An offensive lob hit top-spin to bound away from the base line is a very lethal weapon. Figure 17 shows the use of the defensive lob. The lob is probably the most under-used of the recommended service returns in championship and, particularly, in weekend play. A perfect defensive lob is a thing of beauty, as effective as any return—practice getting the ball as close to the base line as possible.

To become the perfect receiver requires one additional skill: disguising your return. As one of the greatest doubles players of all time stated it: "Few of us can break serve through sheer power of returns. I suggest that, like a baseball pitcher who throws his fast ball, curve, and change-of-pace ball all with the same motion, the tennis player learn to make a drive, a lob, and a soft, tantalizing shot, as the baseball pitcher, with the same motion. With control, and these three shots well disguised, the receiver will find it considerably easier to dislodge the opponents from the advantageous net position." Concealment, surprise, and variety are the hallmarks of the great receivers.

The Importance of the Receiver Taking Net

In order to impress upon the receiver the importance of following his return in to net, we collected a large quantity of data on the subject. To make it more meaningful we omitted all points where aces were served or where the return was an error. Thus, the contest became a duel be-

Figure 18

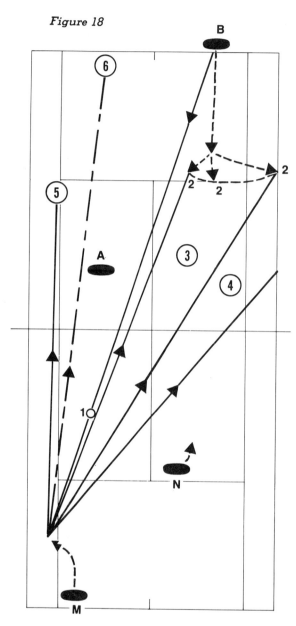

RETURNS OF SHALLOW SERVES IN DOUBLES

The shallow serve is the receiver's delight, as it permits him a good opportunity to win the point.

The receiver moves forward as the serve lands shallow at point 1 and has the opportunity to select a variety of returns. He can catch server B way back near the service line by driving to his feet at point 2 in area 3, or can play a sharply angled return to area 4 for a possible winner.

The other openings include driving down the line to area 5 if net man A moves to cover the center, or playing an offensive lob over net man A to area 6. Often, by dropping back a step or two, the receiver can entice the server into running in too close to the net. This allows the receiver to hit a more effective offensive lob over the head of the surprised server.

Some players try to rattle the server on second serves by moving forward and ready to hit a favorite return. Such tactics do draw some double faults as well as shallow serves.

tween the receiver who had made a successful return, his partner, and the serving team.

On an overall basis the serving team wins a little over 60 percent of points after a successful return of service. However, if the receiver can make a successful return of service which also permits him and his partner to run in to the net position, the receiving team wins 50 percent of the time. Good players can follow 30 to 50 percent of successful returns in to net, particularly behind dinks and top-spin drives which force the server to volley up. The chances of advancing to the net behind the return are six times greater on the second serve, which usually lands less deep in the service court, permitting the wise receiver to move in, drive offensively, and gain a few steps on his journey to net.

There is no doubt that the receiver has every incentive to learn how to execute his tactics so that a quick advance to the net becomes second nature.

If a server is thrown off balance, or is old, tired, or lazy, he may fail to follow his service in to the net. The alert receiver, immediately aware of the lapse, should alter his tactics to take maximum advantage of it. Here the dink and short-topped drive are not so effective: either shot would allow the server to correct his mistake by moving up to play a ground stroke from near the service line, where he could make an offensive shot and finally gain his proper position at net. Instead, the receiver should hit a deep cross-court drive or, better yet, a deep down-the-middle shot (taking the angle away) which will hold the server in the back court, and follow his drive rapidly in to the net. Other good strokes to use are sliced or chopped shots hit to an area deeper than the service court. Preferably, these strokes should have a low bounce, so that the server is forced to dig them up for a weak return. Any one of these strokes will force a defensive return by the server; and with one man up and one back, the ranks of the serving team can be pierced through the open diagonal. This play (illustrated in Figure 62) is fundamental and should be an old story to doubles players by this time.

Modified Net-Man Tactics

Rather than play beside the receiver on the base line, the recommended position for his partner was shown in the modified net position in Figure 8. From this area it is much easier for the receiving team to coordinate in capturing the offensive, as we shall see.

The modified net man should base his play on the three following rules:

1. He must anticipate.

To the uninitiated player, it may seem at first that to play the modified net position is to flirt unnecessarily with injury. After all, the opponents at net can slam any high ball right into your stomach with the speed and force of a boxer's left hand. Maybe the Doherty brothers shouldn't have invented this exposed front-line position!

Well, the risk isn't as great as it may seem. The modified net man can learn to anticipate the intentions of the opponents rather easily, and once he has learned, he can not only defend himself effectively, but also take the offense quite often.

Anticipating in the modified net position requires a routine. The player should stand slightly sideways to the net, facing toward the opposing net man A. As the serve is hit, he should watch the ball only long enough to note the start of the return of the service. Then he will know reasonably well the type and direction of return, and what to expect on the first volley of the serving team. Immediately he should shift his attention *ahead* of the ball to opposing net man A. By watching him for an instant, he can discover any intention of the net man to intercept the return. If it is apparent that the opposing net man will not play the shot, the modified net man should continue to turn his eyes and body ahead of the ball toward the advancing server, to learn his position and the type of volley he is getting set to play. Thus, a quick sweep of the court, from receiver to net man to advancing server, tells the modified net man who will make the first volley. Then he should study the man about to hit the volley to anticipate accurately the type and direction of the shot. If the club player finds that he cannot keep up with such speedy, complex action, he should skip watching the receiver and concentrate on whether or not the net man will play the shot. He can turn to watch the advancing server an instant later.

2. He must play his position so as to take advantage of weak first volleys by the serving team.

Remember, the receiving team must take the offensive if it is to break service, and the recommended returns of service all work toward this end. Also remember that it is difficult for the receiver to force a weak volley on his return of service. So it becomes imperative that the receiving team be in a position to exploit every poor first volley.

The position of modified net man N is selected in part for just this purpose. He is close enough to the net to move in rapidly and hit down a defensive first volley hit up by the serving team. He is located near the center of the court because the server, volleying a good return of service from close to the ground, will usually hit it cross court over the lowest part of the net; and player N has to move only a few feet to intercept the shot. It is also possible for player N to reach a volley hit down the line—because down-the-line volleys are hit up somewhat to clear the high portion of the net, and rather softly to keep them from sailing over the base line. Of course, the modified net man has to antici-pate the direction of the server's first volley and get a good jump on the ball (just like a good shortstop in baseball).

Typical points won by an alert modified net man are shown in Fig-ures 19 and 20. It is sound tennis for player N to take chances by edging toward the center and preparing to poach when his partner makes an effective return of service. The Australians, with their quick-on-the-trig-ger anticipation, are particularly adept at poaching for a kill. The exact position of the modified net player is determined by his reach, agility, powers of anticipation, and by the effectiveness of his partner's return of service. Long, lanky players stand way in at times—eight feet from the net and five feet from the center line—particularly on second serves.

Obviously, the receiver, as he follows in behind an effective return of service, may also be in a position to put away for a placement a volley hit up by the server. He should generally come up a little wide (as shown in Figure 19) to cover the part of the net his partner cannot reach.

3. He must play his position so that he can make an adequate shot even though badly exposed through a mediocre return of service by his partner.

Since a well-played return of service is difficult to make, the initial position of player N is based in part on the assumption that the return of service may be weak. If the return *is* weak, he will need time as well as anticipation. Anticipation has been covered. Player N gains a mo-ment by locating himself just inside the service line, rather than close to the net where he could be volleyed at from point-blank range. His posi-tion near the line separating the service courts enables him to cover volleys struck by either the server or the net man.

Return of Service Against Unconventional Serving Formations

Up to this point all returns of service mentioned or diagrammed have been based on the assumptions that the serving team is using the con-

Figure 19

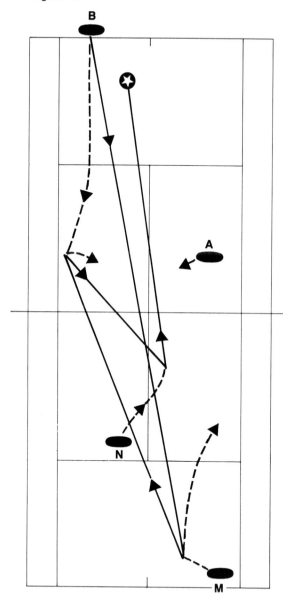

This diagram illustrates exactly why the great doubles teams use the receiving formation which places the partner of the receiver, player N, at the modified net position.

Receiver M has hit a fine backhand cross-court dink return of service which should force server B to volley up. Modified net player N, in carrying out his responsibilities, notes the type of return his partner has hit, sees that net man A is not poaching, and then detects that server B will have a tough time volleying the return of service. Upon anticipating that server B will probably have to volley up cross court, modified net player N moves forward and then, when player B is committed, poaches to volley down the center for an easy placement.

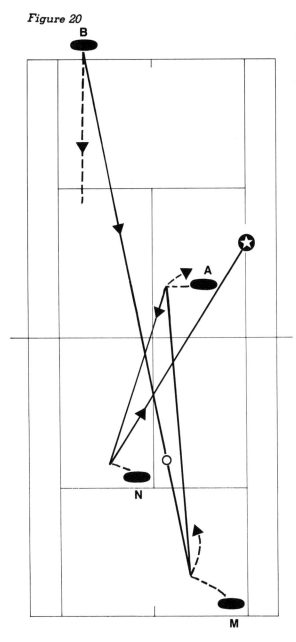

Figure 20

B

N

M

DEFENSIVE MODIFIED NET PLAY

The play depicted here is a perfect example of why the modified net player is instructed to sweep the court with his eyes on each return, noting his partner's stroke, the opposing net player's moves, and the position of the next shot being made by the net-rushing server.

In this instance receiver M has played a weak return which modified net player N judges will be intercepted by net man A for an apparent easy winner. However, player N watches very carefully the position of player A's backswing, racket, and body and is able to anticipate a hard volley aimed toward his backhand. A step in the proper direction and a quick reaction result in turning disaster into a magnificent angle-volley placement. That sort of defensive play can break a server's heart—and his service, too.

Figure 21

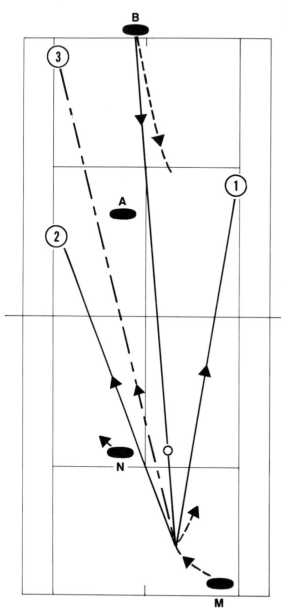

RETURNS OF SERVICE AGAINST UNCONVENTIONAL SERVING FORMATIONS

Figure 21A illustrates the receiver M facing a reverse serving formation. His most effective return is down the line to area 1, or angled behind net man to area 2 if he is too close to the center. Also an effective play is the lob cross court to area 3, which server B has just left.

Figure 21B shows a planned poach by net player A off of the reverse serving formation in order to cut off the down-the-line return to area 1. The counter for this play is to play cross court to area 2 or lob to area 3 the moment you catch player A moving.

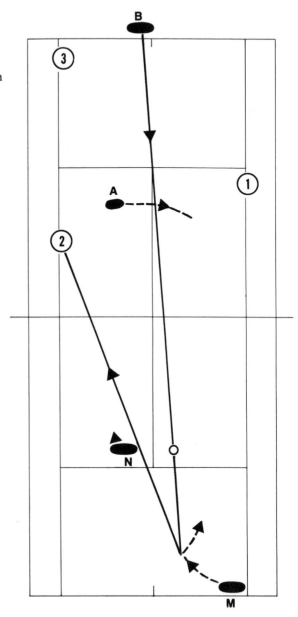

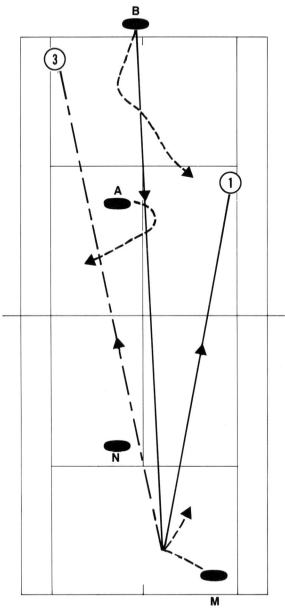

Figure 21C depicts the fake poach by player A. The best answer is to hit down the line to area 1 or lob cross court to area 3.

Figure 21D shows the poach off of the conventional serving formation. The answer if you catch net player A moving is to hit behind him down the line to area 1. If player A is late in starting, the cross-court return to area 2 should beat him.

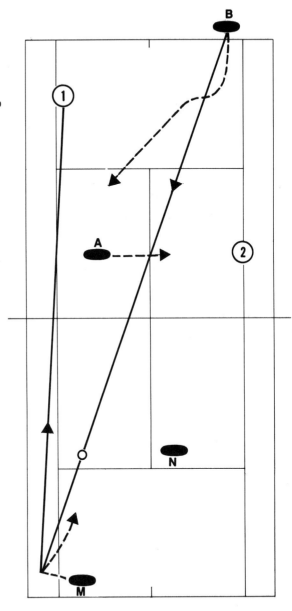

ventional formation (depicted in Figure 8), and that the server is following his service in to the net position in every case. Let us now consider the return of service against unconventional or trick serving formations.

To begin with, the receiver, as he prepares to execute his return, must keep one of his "several" eyes on the serving team in order to detect any rapid change in position. There are several formations and fakes he may have to face. In general, such formations are calculated to rattle, confuse, or surprise the receiver; and they will succeed on all counts unless the receiver is alert and knows what counteraction to take. These formations can be met successfully; otherwise. an unconventional formation would quickly become *the* conventional formation. The proper counterattacks are shown in Figure 21 (see pages 86 to 89).

6

NET PLAY

The ability to play net is absolutely essential to the all-court tennis game required by sound tactics applied to both singles and doubles. Control of the net represents the best attacking position for both games, and the volley and overhead are the knockout blows. Control of the net keeps the opposition on the defensive. In singles on fast courts about 30 to 35 percent of all winners are hit from the net; on slow courts 20 to 25 percent. In doubles the speed of the court has much less effect on tactics, so that about 55 percent of all winners are made from the net position irrespective of court surface. Net play is absolutely essential to satisfactory doubles.

The importance of the volley, overhead, and ground strokes from net position should be abundantly clear to all readers. We recommend that all players practice net play, not just because proficiency at net is vital, but also because the strokes are both fun and thrilling to execute. The younger one learns, of course, the better. Often the budding player growing up on slow courts makes the mistake of failing to master this aspect of the game, which is a great handicap when he or she shifts from time to time into fast-court play. And, unfortunately, many readers know adult players who are almost afraid of having fast balls hit at them in the net position.

Failure to master the volley, which is the stroke most used in net play, is almost a ridiculous shortcoming, since the stroke is easy to produce as soon as one understands the principles involved. We believe a few comments on the volley at this point will assist in the presentation of this chapter as well as your ultimate enjoyment of the game. In short, we intend to make you feel at home at net.

THE FUNDAMENTALS OF VOLLEYING

Body and Racket Position

The proper volley position involves three main basics.

First, the head of the racket must be above the grip. The reason for this is that when the hand is in that position the grip is about 20 percent stronger than when the wrist is extended in a downward position to intercept a ball below the racket head. (Bending the opponent's wrist downward is a favorite method used by wrestlers to break a grip.) To accomplish this racket-head position, it is imperative that the player bend his knees accordingly. A major shortcoming of most weekend players, particularly women, is failure to bend the knees far enough "to get down to the ball" so that the wrist is below the ball. A stronger grip

Figure 22: The Concave Volley Wall

is vital in intercepting hard-driven balls, particularly if they strike the racket slightly off center.

Second, the ball must be struck about twelve inches in front of the body in order to permit the eyes to follow the ball into the center of the racket. It is impossible to turn the head and eyes fast enough to track a high-velocity drive as the ball moves from a point about a foot in front of the player to his side. Attempting to volley the ball at your side only results in off-centered contact between ball and racket and consequent errors. To strike the volley properly in front of the body requires that the wrist be laid back and locked, pointing toward the sideline, in order to present the total racket face to the on-rushing ball.

And, third, the angle of the racket face has to be adjusted to lift the ball over the net from a shoe-top volleying position, to play the ball level from about waist high, and to direct the ball downward from the chest upward. In other words, firm wrist and the racket face must present a solid concave volley wall as depicted in Figure 22. Note how the body is turned sideways to the net, eyes focused on the ball, the wrist is below the racket head and also laid back and locked to present a racket face aimed directly at the oncoming ball.

The Grip and the Stroke

Since the ball travels from base line to net in 0.2 to 0.3 second, it is essential the player be ready to volley instantaneously from either the forehand or the backhand side, or from a position directly in front of the body. To be prepared, two things must be remembered.

First, since there is insufficient time to alter the grip on the racket, a grip which permits equally effective returns from all angles must be adopted. The top players utilize the Continental grip (Figure 3), as it affords the best answer to the all-purpose volley (as well as overhead) grip. The ready position for the volleyer has the weight equally distributed on the balls of the feet, with knees slightly bent and racket in front pointing toward the receiver. It should be cradled lightly near the throat with the left hand to assist in making turns with equal rapidity to either side.

Second, because of the brief time available, the stroke must ordinarily be restricted to a punch shot with a short backswing of one to two feet and a short follow-through with a stiff wrist.

As always, there are certain exceptions to stroking recommendations. When the ball is above the waist and can be hit downward (see

Figure 22), a bigger backswing can be utilized if time is available. This is called a swinging, rather than a punch, volley and is often used in trying to bang placements, particularly when the volleyer is presented with a high sitter.

Anticipation

Once again, the minimal travel time of the ball places burdens upon the singles net player or doubles net team to anticipate the type and direction of the return, otherwise he or they might be caught by surprise and out of position. This is particularly true in doubles when the opponents are in the volleying position and the ball flies back and forth in 0.1 to 0.2 second. As already pointed out in Chapter 2, it is relatively easy to anticipate the intentions of the stroker if you identify the type of return your own shot should elicit, if you study the striker's stroking habits, and also the position of his feet, body, arm, backswing, and racket as he begins to execute his return.

With practice, these seemingly complex and interrelated giveaway factors can be diagnosed at a glance. This permits, in turn, a quick shift of position to intercept the anticipated return skillfully and to gain the split-second time advantage necessary to the planning, selection, and execution of an effective offensive answer.

Practicing volleying can be great fun. The best procedure is to position a player on each side of the net just in front of the point where the three service-court lines come together, which is known as the T. From these deep positions each player is forced to learn how to bend down to hit the more difficult, low volleys. Top doubles players can keep the ball flying back and forth low over the net for minutes at a time. The importance of keeping the ball low should be obvious: it prevents the opponent from hitting down a severe, offensive volley for a likely winner.

Moving to the Proper Position

In addition to being ever alert with the brain ticking, balance perfect, and reflexes sharp, the accomplished net player must understand how to move to the proper position at the right moment. This is a complex subject in which singles and doubles tactics differ completely. Therefore, these aspects of net play will be treated separately in the text which follows in this chapter.

SINGLES NET-PLAY BASICS

Net play in singles should be thought of as involving two consecutive strokes: a forcing approach shot to set the stage for the trip from the base line to the net, and a follow-up shot to be played from the net position. For the net shot to be a winner, the approach shot must be effective in forcing a defensive reply. A weakness prevalent among many players is the tendency to rush the net despite having executed a weak approach shot. If you then proceed to lose the point, it should probably be blamed more on the non-forcing approach shot than on your inability to volley. Practice in developing good forcing shots which will drive the opponent off balance is an essential part of the volleying game which is all too often overlooked.

To become a good net player it is necessary to learn the following: (1) how to acquire the net position, (2) proper volleying positions and anticipation of the opponent's return, and (3) proper placing of net shots. These factors will be presented in order.

Getting to the Net

A player should run to the net only after preparing the way by means of a shot which is expected to force a defensive return by the opponent. There are essentially four types of approach shots which can open up an opportunity for capturing the net position:

1. A forcing serve
2. A forcing return of service
3. A forcing ground stroke made from any shallow return—that is, from a ball bouncing more than about ten feet inside your base line
4. An offensive lob

These four approach methods will now be analyzed.

For a serve to be sufficiently forcing to provide you with an acceptable chance of making a telling first volley, it must be hit deep on a fast court. Against most players the deep serve should be directed to the outside corner to open up the court for a cross-court volley, or to the backhand corner to draw a weaker return, as previously shown in Figure 7A.

The proper path of the server in running rapidly to the net position depends on the bounce point of the serve, as depicted in Figure 23.

Figure 23

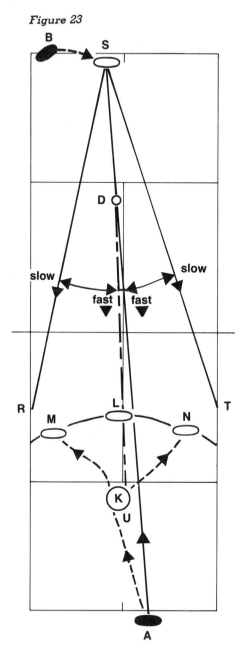

CAPTURING THE NET BEHIND SERVE

This Figure shows two standard methods of taking the net behind serve.

Figure 23A depicts the best simple approach to the net when the serve is directed toward point D, deep and near the center of the court. This restricts the possible angle of receiver B's return to RST, the bisector of which is SU. The best path for the server to the net is just inches on the down-the-line side of SU, since a slightly faster return can be hit down that side and still remain in the court. The server, on running in, pauses momentarily for a balanced hop at point K, and then moves toward point L, M, or N, depending on the anticipated direction of the return of service. Note that for every foot closer to the net along the K to L line, the server gains by having about one less foot width of court to cover on either side. Returns wide to the sidelines toward point R or T can ordinarily be intercepted because they must be hit slowly, as indicated, or sail beyond the sideline.

Figure 23B shows the proper, more complex approach to the net following a serve wide to the backhand corner. When receiver B moves to point E, he enjoys a wider effective angle of return, DEF, the bisector of which is EG. While the return cross court to D has to be hit slowly to stay in the court, the down-the-line shot toward point F can be struck with blistering speed. This means that the server, in trying to plan his approach to the net, must favor the down-the-line side of the bisector to hop point K, and then on to point L, M, or N as anticipated.

These two diagrams serve to illustrate the difference between the so-called center theory and the corner theory. The center theory, as shown in Figure 23A, restricts the receiver to a smaller angle for a passing shot against the advancing server, but does place the receiver in a better position to return any answering volley because he is already well located at the center of the base line. The corner theory, as shown in Figure 23B, drives the receiver off the court, but does provide him with the advantage of a wider offensive angle for return of service. However, this type of serve also opens up the court for a possible easy winning cross-court volley by the server.

The duel between server and receiver over which will win with center-theory or corner-theory tactics is continuous. Anticipation, severity, speed, variety, deception, and other factors will determine the ultimate victor in each match.

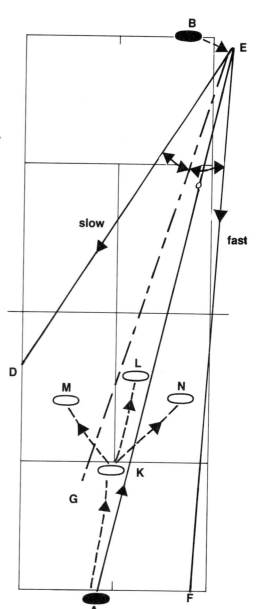

Figure 24

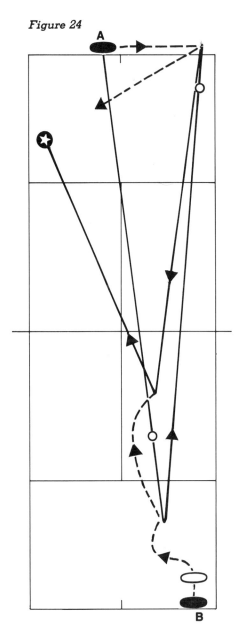

GOING TO NET BEHIND RETURN OF SERVICE

Since the odds of winning a particular point favor the server, any possible opportunity to steal away the offense must be grabbed by the receiver.

In this diagram receiver B has elected to move in a couple of steps because server A has just missed his first serve. This simple move exerts psychological pressure on the server, as he senses that the receiver may try to take away the offense. Indeed, receiver B does just that by continuing forward, running around the shallow second serve, driving a forehand deep down the line, and rushing to the net. The server, pinned in the back court, has to reach for the ball and can only try to pass down the line. Receiver B anticipated this, moves to his right, and is rewarded with an easy angle volley for the point.

This sort of maneuver represents an invaluable method for breaking serve. All players should master this sequence.

There is no time to linger, as with every foot the server can get closer to the net, the more he cuts down the receiver's passing angle, and the less likely he will have to play the volley from the vulnerable "at the feet" position shown. Of course, you cannot be too headlong in your dash to the net or you will invite an offensive lob.

Since there is room for the receiver to pass the advancing server if he is a step out of position, it behooves the server to study the patterns of service returns utilized by his opponent. For example, it was noted in Figures 10 and 11 that the preponderance of deep serves are returned cross court, particularly from the backhand side, and shallow serves tend to be hit down the line.

In capturing the net on return of service it is best to wait for a second serve, which is usually less severe and shallower than the first serve (see Figure 24). Many a fast-court championship match has turned on this tactic. Once one of the contestants starts to miss his first serve you can see his opponent sense the opening, begin to move forward, and play for the all-important service break. Camping on the weak second serve is a favorite maneuver for women and men receivers on both fast and slow surfaces.

Some of the most picture-perfect strokes in tennis, and certainly the most used method of gaining the net position in singles, are the attacking ground strokes. Such approach shots cannot be made from the base line because the run to the net is too long. Instead, about 90 percent of the time such journeys to the net are engineered by taking advantage of a shallow return by the opponent. In essence, most base-line exchanges have as their goal forcing the opponent into making an error or a weak return. Once you have extracted a shallow return, landing ten or more feet inside the base line, you must learn to capitalize on the situation. This calls for moving forward to play the ball near the top of the bounce, hitting a forcing shot, usually down the line, and continuing your forward movement into the volleying position. Many weekend players do not utilize proper tactics in executing this approach shot. The correct tactics are explained in Figure 25.

The final method of gaining the net is by means of an offensive lob. Once again, the approach shot is best made after a shallow return, such as a weak volley, as depicted in Figure 26. This lob requires good control, as if hit too high it might sail out, and if too low could permit the opponent to jump and and reverse the outcome with a winning overhead.

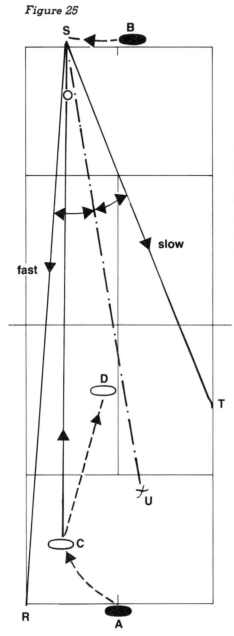

Figure 25

GOING TO NET BEHIND A GROUND STROKE

These diagrams illustrate the tactics to be employed in taking the net behind a ground stroke following a shallow return by your opponent to point C.

Figure 25A shows the manner utilized by most top players. Player A moves forward from the ready position to hit the approach shot down the line deep and runs in rapidly to point D on the down-the-line side of bisector SU of the possible angle of return RST. This means that player A has had to run the minimum distance to reach the optimum volleying position to defend against the potentially faster down-the-line return.

Figure 25B illustrates the method of approach often used by weekend players. They are liable to choose the cross-court return in order to try to take advantage of the normally weaker backhand capabilities of most opponents. However, this means that player A has to run four to five feet farther to reach the optimum volleying position at point D. Were opponent B a top player, he would have time to whip a passing shot down the line along ST. This is the reason the professionals seldom use the cross-court approach shot.

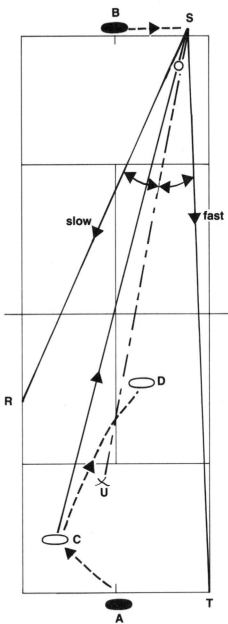

Figure 26

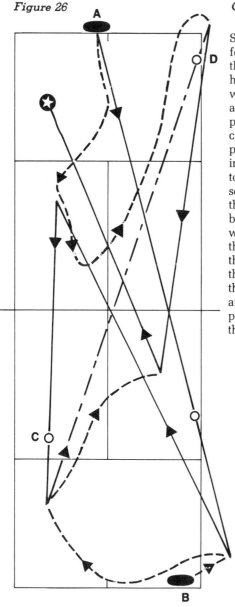

GOING TO NET BEHIND A LOB

Server A has served wide to the forehand and taken the net to volley the cross-court return. However, he has hit up a shallow volley to point C which receiver B immediately notes and changes direction to cover. As he proceeds he glimpses his opponent continuing toward the net position. The picture of an offensive lob appears instantly on his mind, and he decides to deliver an arched shot safely over server A deep to point D. In playing the lob he is careful to aim it over A's backhand side where the overhead is weaker, as well as cross court where the safe distance is longer. This forces the server to reverse his tracks to cover the lob. As he does so, receiver B grabs the opportunity to take the offensive and move in to net. This tactic proves profitable, as B is able to angle-volley the return for a winner.

Proper Volleying Positions and Anticipation

Assuming you have now been able to gain the net position by any one of the four methods outlined, the tactics of net play itself become important.

The proper volleying position at net is that point on the court which gives you the best chance of playing offensively your opponent's return. To volley offensively, it is best to be close to the net in order to hit down on the ball. But you cannot move in too close, lest you be lobbed. The best compromise is to stand six to ten feet from the net, depending in part on your height and agility. This means that the proper volleying position for most players is in the center of the court astride the line that divides the service courts at a point six to ten feet from the net. We will refer to this as the basic volleying position.

But you cannot take for granted that once you have reached the basic volleying position you can afford to remain glued to that spot. On the contrary, you must realize that your opponent has a good chance of passing you from almost any location on the court. Therefore, it is essential that you anticipate the type and direction of the passing shot which is about to be fired against you and move to meet the ball, or you stand to lose the point.

As pointed out briefly in Chapter 2, the ability to achieve anticipation is an art which entails four parts. Nowhere is the need to be able to execute these four steps rapidly and effectively more important than in the situation when play is one-on-one near the net. Two examples of the fantastic anticipation exhibited by top players are shown in Figure 27. Remember that to anticipate you must violate one of the cardinal rules of tennis: you have to take your eye off of the ball and study your opponent to diagnose the type and direction of his shot.

Placing Volleys and Overheads

Once you attain the net, the experts all agree on two tactics. First, you have to go for the kill, or you invite being passed on the return. And, second, if you are forced to hit up a defensive volley, hit it deep. This allows you time to get back to the basic volleying position and keeps the opponent pinned back where his passing shot is least effective. Remembering and carrying out these two commandments will go a long way toward making your net play effective.

If the server follows his serve to net and volleys the return of service, we call this a first volley. Any other volleys are referred to as later

Figure 27

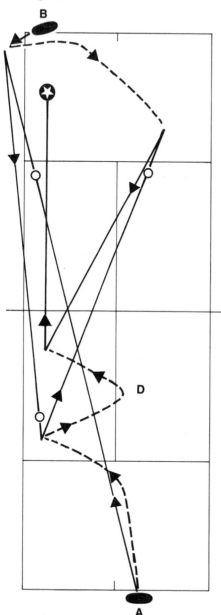

ANTICIPATION IN ACTION

Figure 27A shows a good wide serve to the forehand by player A being returned beautifully down the line by receiver B. Server A is barely able to return a half volley rather feebly cross court. This presents receiver B with an excellent down-the-line passing opportunity. In this desperate situation server A starts to cover the expected down-the-line passing shot by running toward the sideline. However, as he moves he studies his opponent's intentions and notes that he is preparing to reach out and roll over the ball to make a cross-court return, rather than slicing it down the line. In order to camouflage the fact he has anticipated the shot, player A takes one deceptive step over the center line at point D, then reverses direction rapidly and sprints to his left. At the last moment his quick reflexes produce a great saving volley and turn a losing predicament into a winner.

In Figure 27B player A attempts to pass player B, who has volleyed short. Assuming that his passing shot will force an error or weak return, player A elects to move in behind it toward the net. However, alert player B is able to cover the shot as he moves left from the basic volleying position. Player A notes this and realizes he is moving into an almost impossible defensive position as he continues to run to net. En route he studies intently his opponent's stroke preparation, and diagnoses that B will be hitting the volley in front of his body and swinging from the sideline to direct the ball cross court. Thus, player A pauses a split second at point M to hide his intentions until player B is fully committed. Then he switches his attention from his opponent's stroke-preparation motions to focus his eyes upon the ball, dashes across the court, and lunges to intercept the ball. This results in an unbelievable volley winner down the line—while thus stretched out at full length, this was clearly the only place he could direct the shot.

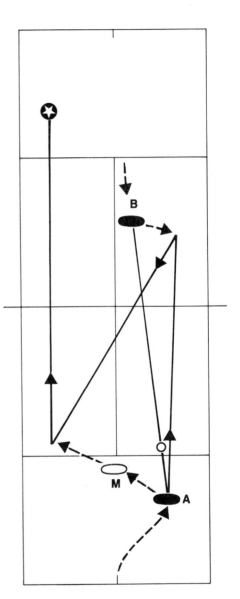

Figure 28

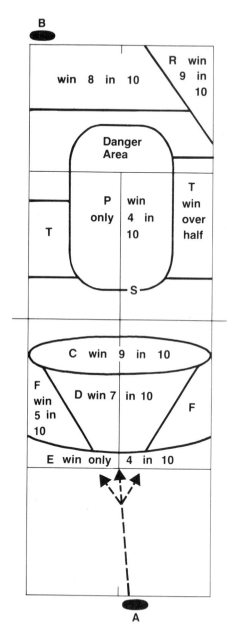

COMPOSITE PICTURE OF FIRST-VOLLEY TACTICS WHEN SERVING TO THE FOREHAND COURT

The lower portion of the diagram shows first-volley positions. The most important thing to recognize is that the closer in to net the server can penetrate, the better his chances of winning the point. As indicated, if you can advance all the way in to area C, you should be able to win in nine cases out of ten because you are in position to volley the ball down or angle it severely (naturally, you also have to be prepared to reverse to cover a lob). From slightly deeper in area D you ordinarily win seven in ten times. If you are forced out of position and wide by a good return of service to either area F, your chances of winning fall to even. And if your run to the net is slow, you end up in area E hitting lots of volleys up from your shoe tops and losing six out of ten points.

The upper portion of the figure depicts the outcome of points played depending on the landing area of the first volley. By all means you must avoid dumping a short volley into Danger Area P, as you stand to lose 60 percent of points because you have presented the receiver with a great passing-shot opportunity. The primary objective of the volleyer is to hit the ball deep to area Q or R (within ten feet of the base line), because you should wind up winning about eight out of ten times. If you utilize the favorite tactic of serving wide to pull the receiver off court and then volleying deep into the opposite corner to area R, you should win 90 percent of the time. Angle volleys to areas T win more than half the time (the T area is longer on the backhand side when serving to the forehand court). Drop volleys into area S require great touch to produce winners and are usually effective only when made from area C.

Tactics for serves to the backhand court are a mirror image of those here represented for the forehand court.

volleys. The first volley is often classified as the most important volley. This is because it is the most difficult volley to play, and also because it sets the stage for the ultimate outcome of the point. To understand the tactics for positions from which to make the first volley and the preferred aim points, we studied hundreds of first volleys and the resulting points as played by numerous world-class players. From the data there emerged a clear pattern of how points are won or lost. A summary diagram showing the positions and outcomes of first-volley points is presented in Figure 28. It is difficult to overemphasize the importance to the singles player of having this picture stamped upon his or her memory.

Later volleys, already defined as any volleys hit following a first volley off return of service, win more points than first volleys. This is particularly true on slow courts and in women's tennis, where the server is less overpowering. Once again, the recommended volley tactic is to go for the kill. This usually means playing to the open part of the court, hitting behind or "wrong-footing" the opponent, or deceiving your antagonist by faking one type of volley and then changing direction or speed or both at the last moment. If you cannot decide what to do, volley deep so you can get another chance. The closer you can get to the net, the more offensive the volley can be—but you have to remain alert to a possible lob. Some later volley situations are described in Figure 29.

DOUBLES NET-PLAY BASICS

Net play completely dominates the game of doubles because over half of all points are won at the net. Since only about one fourth of all points are won from the base line, this means that the net position enjoys a two-to-one advantage over the base-line position. And if you exclude the serve and return of service, which must be played from the base line, the advantage of the net position over the base-line position increases to a staggering three to one! This is confirmed in Table 7, which shows the overwhelming potency of the overhead and volley compared to other strokes.

It is obvious that the net position must be captured at all costs. It is equally apparent that the accomplished doubles player must understand thoroughly the tactics of net play. Such comprehension involves mastery of the following: (1) methods of capturing the net position, (2)

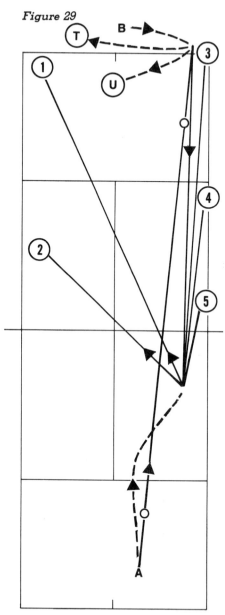

Figure 29

PLACING THE VOLLEY

Player A has taken the net, in Figure
29A, behind a forcing ground stroke
down the line to the backhand to put
him in position for a later volley. The
diagram begins with opponent B
attempting a passing shot down the
line. This establishes a series of tactical
choices for volleyer A. Under most
circumstances the proper shot is to aim
point 1 in the opposite corner, as it
forces player B to make a long run and
keeps him back on the base line. If the
attempted passing shot is high, volleyer
A should move forward and angle-·
volley down sharply to aim point 2 for
an easy placement. Other alternatives
are presented if opponent B is running
hard at point T or U toward the
expected aim points 1 and 2. Under
these circumstances the volleyer has
three possible aim points, all of which
attempt to "wrong-foot" player B. This
means hitting behind player B so that
he cannot reverse direction rapidly
enough to retrieve the ball. As shown,
aim points 3 and 4 are the logical
places to put the ball out of reach
behind an off-balance opponent. Either
shot can be assisted by pretending first
to hit cross court before dumping the
ball down the line. Finally, a clean
placement can be achieved by a
delicate drop volley to aim point 5.
The risk here is that drop volleys are
difficult to execute both well and
consistently.

Figure 29B shows what happens when volleyer A has made the tactical mistake of hitting a shallow and tentative cross-court volley. This gives player B an opportunity to pass the volleyer. If player A has only reached the service line at about point T, player B can pass down the line. If player A has moved fast to reach point U and his momentum is carrying him toward the sideline, player B can hit behind him with a top-spin forehand.

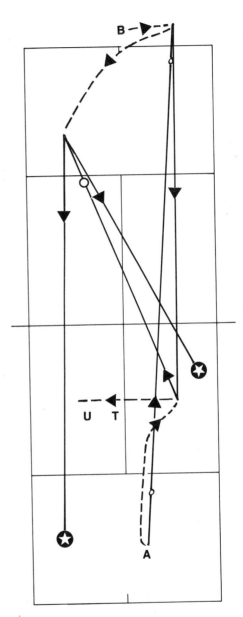

team volleying positions, (3) anticipation of opponent's returns, and (4) selection and placing of net shots. We will explore these four subjects.

Capturing the Net Position

In doubles there are four methods of getting to the net position: (1) behind a serve, (2) behind a return of service, (3) behind a ground stroke, and (4) behind an offensive lob.

As pointed out in Chapter 3, competent women and men doubles players use the serve as a means of gaining the net on every point, irrespective of court surface. The first service offers by far the safer journey, as the receiver normally has to play the return from deep in the court. Even though the receiver can move forward on a second serve and play a more offensive return, the server should take the chance of coming in and playing a more difficult first volley because of the great advantage offered by the net position. Thus, the preferred tactics are to keep each serve deep, and take the net behind every serve.

But there are always exceptions to any tactical rule. Some players do not possess a serve of sufficient severity and depth to permit a safe journey to the net. These players must plan to get to net as soon as possible using one of the remaining methods of so doing.

The strokes for moving to net behind a return of service have been described in Chapter 4. Taking net is a difficult maneuver on a return of a first serve, but is a recommended tactic on a second serve, particularly if it is shallow. A low cross-court return which forces the server to volley up or a lob over the net man, provides the best opportunities to advance. There is a real incentive to do so because it changes the odds of your winning the point from against to even.

Often in doubles one team has either one or two players on the base line trying to escape from that clearly unenviable position. The usual path to the net follows an exchange of shots or fencing period aimed at forcing the opponents to hit a short volley. At that moment the striker and partner must play the proper approach shot and advance to the net position. There are three types of such shots: a low, soft shot which forces a net player to volley up defensively; a hard, low or top-spin drive toward an opening aimed at drawing a weak reply or error: or an offensive lob to the base line (see Figures 58, 61, and 63).

The offensive lob, as already noted, can be used after any short ball, whether a serve or volley, particularly if either net player is crowding the net.

Anticipation and Proper Volleying Positions

The basic volleying position for doubles is shown in Figure 30. It is the best position under normal circumstances and should be reassumed after each stroke unless conditions dictate a realignment. A typical need for readjustment is also shown in Figure 30.

Circumstances other than returns from wide angles which force a modification of the basic volleying position are:

1. If the opponents are about to drive from deep in the court, or if they have to hit up a weak return, the net team can move a step closer to the net in order to be able to volley down.

2. If the opponents also advance to net, it is wise to move in and crowd the center a bit, as this increases the chances of volleying down at their feet without jeopardizing the defense.

3. During rapid exchanges at net a member of the team may anticipate a return and move to intercept the ball to make the kill.

4. Should your partner be forced out of position, such as toward the sideline, you must move a step or so to cover the center.

5. If the opponents are about to lob, both partners should drop back a step or two and prepare to hit an overhead.

In addition to proper position play at net, it is imperative that the partners develop a complete understanding of team play. Only many hours of practice and playing together can build the type of teamwork that permits each player to know who will play the fast-approaching ball, what type of stroke the striker will probably make, where he is most likely to aim the ball, and where he will position himself so that you can anticipate the probable return and move to the spot which places your team in the optimum position. Nothing makes a team feel more stupid than an Alphonse-and-Gaston act, when both partners are within reach of the ball only to let it sail between them for a placement. Each team must evolve its own procedures, but here are six general rules for coordinated net play:

1. A ball hit straight down the center should normally be taken by the player with his forehand toward the center. With two right-handed players, this means the person in the backhand court.

2. If a ball is hit cross court between the net players, it should be taken by the player farther away in the cross-court position. The reasoning is simple. The player on the cross-court side has more time to make his shot, and the ball is coming directly toward his racket. On the other hand, the ball travels past the player on the down-the-line side sooner and at a wider angle which makes it more difficult to volley.

Figure 30

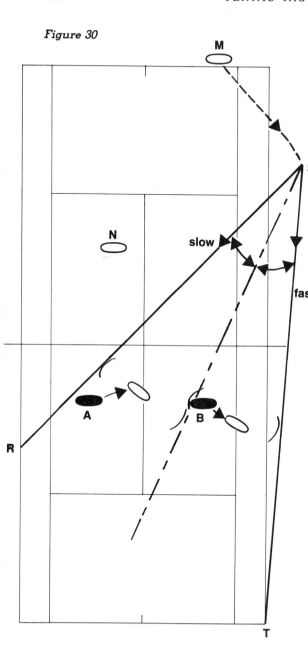

BASIC NET POSITION AND ADJUSTMENTS

The best basic net position is shown by the initial dark positioning of players A and B. Each is about eight feet from the net and from the center service line, and about ten feet from the sideline. If you cannot cover lobs from this position, you can move a bit farther back from the net. This basic position packs the more dangerous center where hard drives pass over the lowest part of the net. Angled shots toward the sideline can be covered, as they have to be hit slower and higher.

When opponent M has to play a ground stroke from point wide of the court, the fast down-the-line shot toward T would be wide open if the net team did not adjust positions. As illustrated, player B has to move back and to the right to cover the alley, and player A has to move forward and to the right to cover the center and the slower angled cross-court return. The net team now presents a solid defense, as shown by the parentheses indicating the range of each player. Should player M lob, the partners should avoid misunderstandings by calling for the ball.

3. During a rapid exchange at point-blank range at net, it is often best for the player who last hit the ball to take shots returned down the middle. This is because he knows where he is placing the ball and should be able to anticipate the return more quickly than his partner.

4. Lobs hit down the middle should be smashed by the player with the forehand in the center. Otherwise, each player should be responsible for lobs on his side.

5. When in doubt, partners should call "Yours" or "Mine." Often a player is caught on the wrong foot or off balance so that he must alert his partner to cover the ball, or he senses an opportunity for a kill and wants to move in front of his partner while avoiding a collision.

6. On returns of service hit down the center the net man usually moves to the middle to try to volley the ball away. The server in moving toward the basic volley position should be prepared to back him up, for often at the last moment the net man will find he cannot reach the ball or play it effectively and will let it go by. In such an emergency he should duck out of the way to give his partner a better chance to make a difficult volley.

Net-Play Tactics

Up to this point we have been laying the groundwork and setting forth the fundamentals for sound doubles play. With all the mechanics firmly in mind, you should now be ready to take up the most interesting and exciting part of doubles: the tactics of actual net play.

Net play starts—logically enough—with the first volley by the serving team. This volley is usually made by the server, since, as we noted in Chapter 4, about 85 percent of all returns of serve are hit cross court at the server as he runs in to net.

The server must recognize that his first volley is the most difficult one for him to make, as well as the most important. After a successful return of service, over one half of the points won by the serving team are won by the first volley stroke itself, and some additional points are won because a strong first volley sets the stage for a later, ultimate winner. However, the serving team has to realize that after a successful return of service its chances of winning the point drop from about 2 to 1 to 1.2 to 1 over the receiving team. All of this means that the server must concentrate on bending his knees and getting down to the ball (most first volleys are hit from near the ground fairly deep in the service court) in order to play the volley carefully.

There are essentially two defensive formations that may greet the server as he starts to make his first volley. As illustrated in Figure 31, they depend on whether the receiver stayed back or followed his return in to net. The proper aim points for each case are shown.

While the server is very busy selecting his first volley, the net man also has responsible duties to perform. He must turn to note the type and direction of the volley about to be made. Then he should rapidly sweep visually the opponent's court, determine the positions of the modified net man and the receiver, anticipate the next shot, and move into the best position. His actions will become clear as we move into complete net-play points.

Points at net require the utmost in tennis courtsmanship, anticipation, deception, patience, agility, and stroke production. It is a game of angles and position which calls for forcing the opponents into the middle and angling off a volley for a placement, or splitting the opposition apart with angles and then volleying down the middle for the point. With all four players at net it is subtle maneuvering for openings, rather than brute force, which wins most points. In general, the team that can play a step closer to the net and force the opposition to volley up has the tactical advantage.

Careful study of the tactics used by the experts, coupled with many hours of playing together, can mold a team which makes the correct shot selection for each situation almost automatically. After all, things are happening so fast you have to make instantaneous decisions. And since your shot selection influences the effectiveness of your partner's positioning and strokes, both players must understand how the team is planning its pattern of shots to win the point.

To assist the reader in grasping the tactics of net play, we have diagrammed a number of points from tournament matches. We have covered all of the different types of strokes. Where possible, we have also presented the diagrams in duplicate, with the proper play for the offensive team on one side and, as nearly as possible, the best counterplay for the defensive team on the other. Finally, we have attempted to avoid cluttering the diagrams by omitting numerous exchanges which led up to the final and deciding thrusts.

The Deep Volley

The crisp, deep volley is a very important stroke in doubles. The reader must realize it wins about twice as many points as any other stroke.

There are logical reasons for this. Since the net is six inches lower in the middle, and the length of court available to the volleyer is about twice as long (for deep volleys) as it is wide (for angle volleys), it is obvious the net player can seek winners hitting severe, low volleys down the middle with less chance of error. A favorite tactic is to divide and conquer by opening up the middle with an angled shot and banging a deep volley down the middle for the point.

A number of examples of deep-volley complete points are presented in Figures 32, 33, 34, and 35.

The Angle Volley

The angle volley is a potent double-duty stroke. Used discriminatingly, it is a subtle weapon for drawing the opponents out of position to establish an opening, as well as being an excellent put-away shot. It is second only to the angled overhead in lethality. This is not surprising because a sharply angled volley must be hit from close to the net, so that it can often be hit down with considerable pace.

In fencing for position with all four players at net the angle volley can serve two purposes. First, in playing a low ball hit at your feet, a soft angle volley hit cross court over the low portion of the net can save you from the tragedy of hitting up toward your opponents. And, second, the striker can often engineer an opening for a deep volley down the center on the next shot. Some typical angle-volley points are shown in Figures 36 and 37.

Sometimes the dink return of service is so expert that a volley return would be too risky, and a ground stroke is preferred. Such a situation is illustrated in Figure 38.

Overhead Play

It is standard practice to place the player with the stronger overhead where his forehand is in the middle so that he can play the majority of lobs, many of which are hit down the center. Other than having this understanding between partners, each player is responsible for lobs hit in his direction in order to maintain proper team position. There are three exceptions to this practice, which, when elected, should be preceded by calls of "Mine" or "Yours" to alert your partner and avoid collisions. First, on short lobs a player may encroach upon his partner's

Figure 31

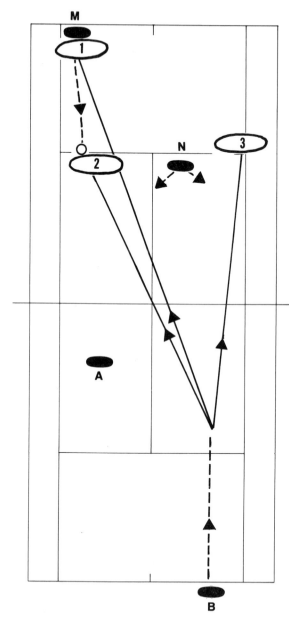

AIM POINTS FOR FIRST VOLLEYS

As a general rule, the server must hit his first volley safely as deep and as near the center of the court as possible in order to attain the most favorable offensive positions. This means hitting the volley to area 1 in Figure 31A if the receiver remains in the back court, and to area 2 if he follows his return in to net. Having to play the return from near the center gives player M the poorest angle for passing. In placing the volley down the center the server has to be wary of possible poaching on the part of modified net man N. To discourage that, it is smart to dump a volley down the line to area 3 from time to time.

Displayed in Figure 31B are aim points when the receiver has hit a weak return which allows server B to move in close to the net. From this position it is relatively easy to hit unanswerable volleys down and severely cross court or down the line as indicated. And if the opponents break toward the sidelines to try to cover the angled shots, a ball struck down the center will produce a winner.

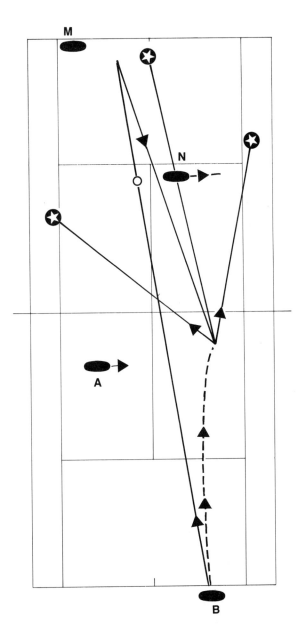

Figure 32

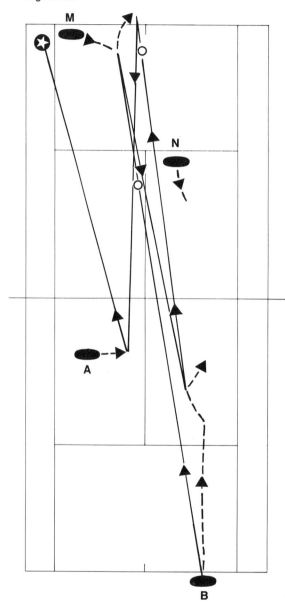

THE DEEP VOLLEY

The point in Figure 32A is a classic sequence which begins with server B making the deep first volley to the center which is recommended by many experts. This keeps receiver M pinned to the base line with the minimum angle for his return. Therefore, the serving team can crowd the center, providing net man A with an easy deep-volley winner.

In Figure 32B server B aims his first volley along the same line, but hits it shallow. This permits receiver M to move forward and play a soft dink down the middle. Recognizing this will force player B to volley up, player M dashes in to the net and punches a deep volley down the line for the point.

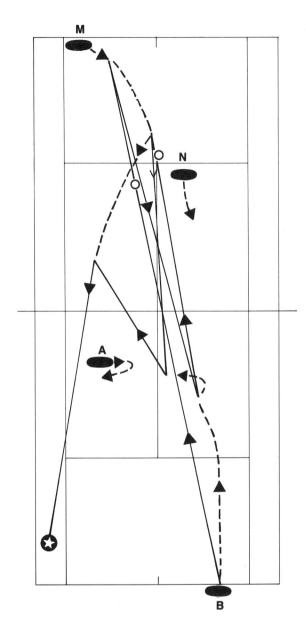

Figure 33

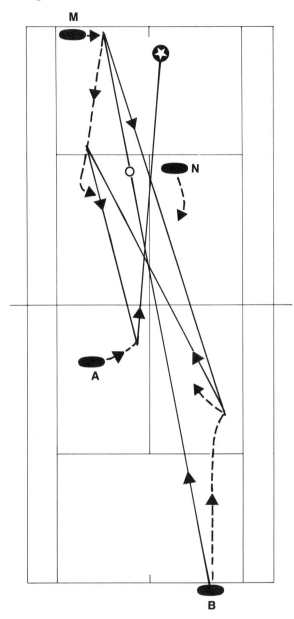

THE DEEP VOLLEY

The play in Figure 33A illustrates server B getting well in to net and making an offensive first volley at the feet of receiver M as he attempts to follow his return in to net. Net man A properly anticipates player M will have to volley up, so he moves over to cut off the return and volleys deep down the middle for an easy point.

Depicted in Figure 33B is a point which begins the same way, but the defense wins out. In this case the server was slower in coming to net and had to volley up from deep in the service court. Receiver M immediately sensed his opportunity and sprinted all out for the net in order to volley deep for a winner.

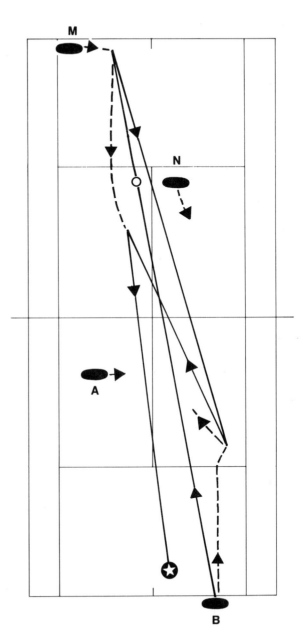

Figure 34

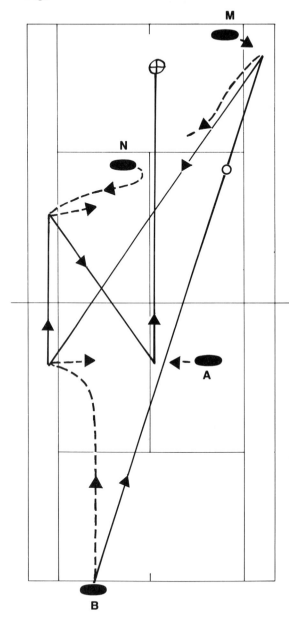

M

N

A

B

THE DEEP VOLLEY

The diagram in Figure 34A shows fine teamwork by the serving team. Receiver M makes an excellent return of service which server B can barely reach after a long run. Modified net man N senses player B will probably have to volley up cross court, which is the normal play, so he takes a step in that direction. Noting this, player B dumps a volley down the line. Since the ball had to be hit up over the highest portion of the net, player N is able to reverse direction, dash over, and barely reach the ball. Net man A now anticipates that player N cannot do much with his volley, so he moves to protect the middle and is rewarded with an easy placement.

In Figure 34B, modified net man N reverses the outcome. This time he anticipates that server B will try to dump a volley behind him down the line, so he fakes by moving straight ahead before swerving and closing rapidly in to net, and volleys deep for a well-earned winner.

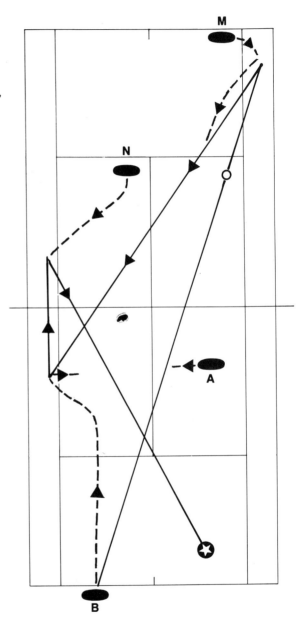

Figure 35

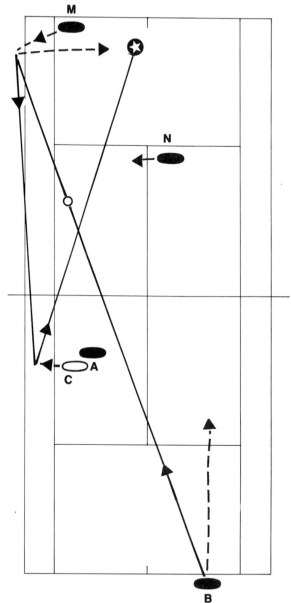

THE DEEP VOLLEY

Figure 35A shows correct net play on the part of net man A. Seeing the serve land wide to pull receiver M off the court, player A wisely moves a step to his left to point C to guard the alley. When he is in fact presented with a return down the sideline, he has to move only a short distance to play a solid deep volley through the open diagonal for the win.

Figure 35B shows what happens if the net man is unprepared. Receiver M notes the unprotected alley and tries to slip a drive down the sideline. Net man A has to dive for the ball and make an ineffective volley. Modified net man N anticipates this and moves rapidly to cut off the shot and volley deep for a nice win.

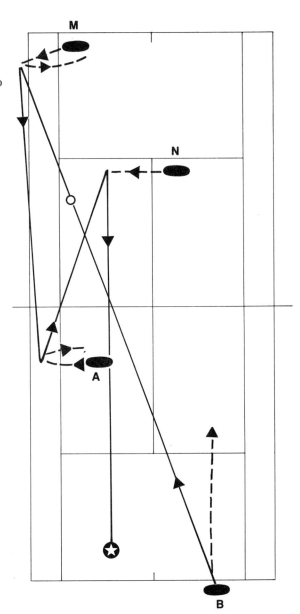

Figure 36

THE ANGLE VOLLEY

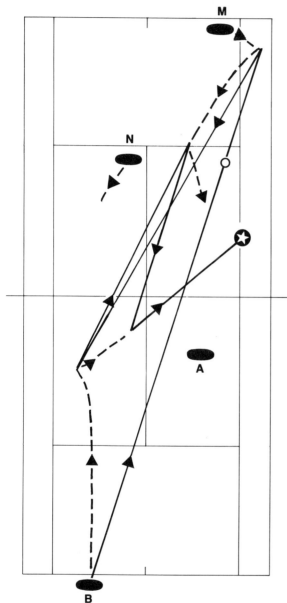

Figure 36A shows a classic angle volley with the stage being set beautifully by server B. First, he follows his serve well in to the net position and volleys offensively down the middle at the feet of advancing receiver M. As he does so, he anticipates that player M will have to volley up. As a result, player B continues moving forward, establishes an offensive position close to the net, and is rewarded by being able to angle-volley an easy placement.

Figure 36B illustrates
essentially the same point with a
different outcome. In this case
server B is slow in following his
serve in to net, so that he has to
volley up defensively from deep
in the service court. This permits
receiver M to move in a step or
two closer and volley softly at
the feet of player B, forcing him
to volley up. Player M continues
to move forward and gains the
opportunity to angle-volley the
return for a placement.

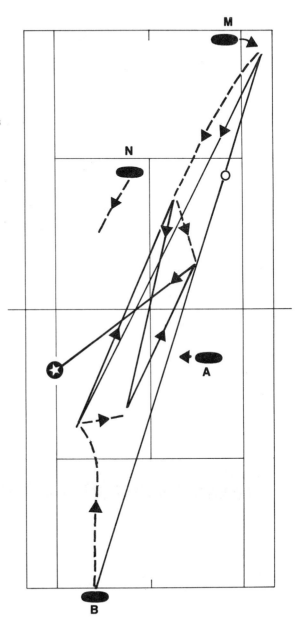

Figure 37

THE ANGLE VOLLEY

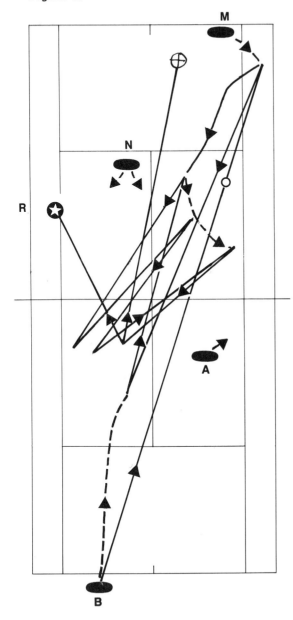

Figure 37A shows a splendid example of a net duel in which soft angle volleys were used to split the defense wide open for the ultimate kill. Receiver M follows his return of service in to net and answers server B's first volley with a soft cross-court volley. This initiates an exchange of two delicate cross-court volleys over the low portion of the net. Meanwhile, net man A guards the alley so player M cannot volley down the line. This opens the way for server B to move in to cut off the cross-court return close to the net and volley it through the opening in the middle for a winner. An alternative volley choice is available, depending on the position of modified net man N. If player N moves to cover the center, player B can angle-volley behind him to point R.

Figure 37B is an excellent play by the receiving team on a shallow serve. Receiver M runs around the serve to hit a top-spin forehand at the feet of server B near the service line. The receiving team sees that player B will have to volley up, so they head for the net. Player M hits a soft volley down the center which net man A has to volley up. Both members of the receiving team pack the center ready for the kill. Modified net man N is in perfect position to angle a winner into the alley.

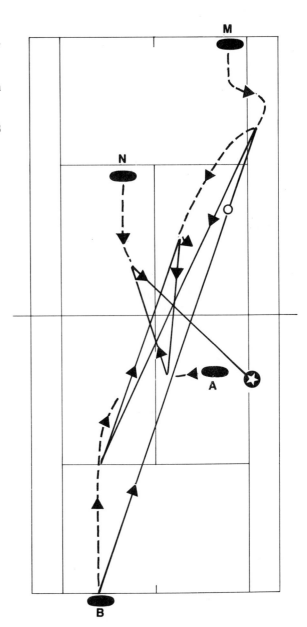

Figure 38

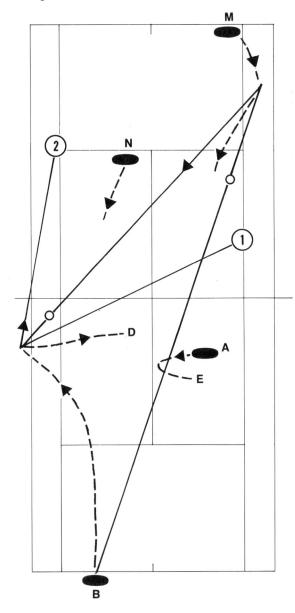

ELECTING NOT TO PLAY THE FIRST VOLLEY

Sometimes it is wise not to play a first volley. This diagram shows a possible answer for the server faced with a near-perfect dink return of service. As server B sprints to try to reach the dink, he realizes any volley would have to be hit up from ground level toward the on-rushing receiving team. Therefore, B slows at the last moment in order to bounce the ball and play a ground stroke. If the bounce is low, he elects to play the ball cross court to area 1 and hurries toward point D while his partner A reverses to point E to establish a defensive alignment. If the bounce is high enough, he can elect to slip a backhand drive down the line to area 2.

court if he happens to be slightly closer to the net or if he can play a sharper-angled overhead for a placement. Second, if one player is caught too close to the net and is about to be lobbed, his partner should drop back to cover behind him. And, third, a bad sun angle or cross-court winds can cause a player to elect to ask his partner to play the shot. Teamwork also calls for a player to call "Bounce it" when he judges a lob is going to float out.

Sound overhead play requires knowledge of the positions of the opponents, skill in concealing the placing of your overhead until the last moment, and a sense for striking the ball hard enough to win the point (or open up the court) but not so violently as to produce an error. The overhead is the most lethal stroke in doubles (Table 8). Consequently, it is most unnerving to have engineered with great precision an opportunity for an easy placement, only to "telegraph" the shot and have it returned, or to blast the shot wide of the court. Forgiveness of flagrant mistakes between partners is a necessary part of team play.

Developing a reliable overhead is of vital importance in doubles. Even though the stroke accounts for only about 14 percent of all winners, its psychological impact is enormous. There is no more pleasurable moment in tennis than smashing away an overhead. It is a stroke which should be practiced. Doubles partners should develop the habit of tossing up lobs to one another to practice lobs as well as overheads, both backhand and forehand, in sun and wind.

The overhead tactics of the great doubles players have been remarkably similar. They play each such point in the surest manner. This entails hitting safe down the center lobs which are deeper than the service line in hopes of drawing a weak return, and going for angled or deep winners when the lob can be struck within the service court. The same tactics apply when a lob must be bounced and struck with a stroke like a serve.

Overhead tactics utilized by the greats are shown in Figures 39 and 40.

The Soft and the Drop Volley

The soft volley is an important stroke because it can be used to draw a weak return. This is accomplished by keeping the ball low to make the opponent volley up, and by slowing the pace of the shot so that the opponent faces a "nothing" ball. Consequently, the soft volley is a favorite shot when all four players are at net jockeying for position. Another use for the soft volley is a defensive one. If you are about to be

Figure 39

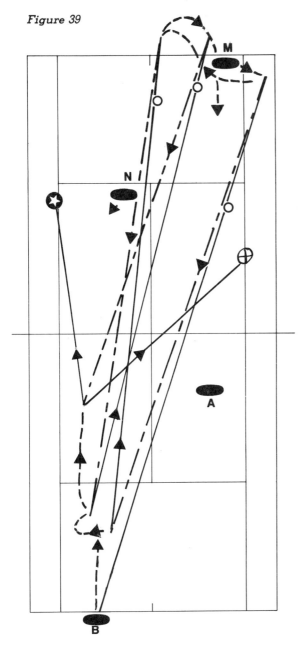

OVERHEAD PLAY

Demonstrated in Figure 39A is a near perfect overhead tactical display by server B. Receiver M lobs the return of service deep, and server B retreats to hit a deep overhead to the middle of the base line which player M retrieves and hits back a second deep lob. Player B again plays a deep overhead to the center to give the defense little angle for an offensive return. This time B draws a short lob inside the service line and moves in to hit the angle overhead to either side for a winner. Care and patience are rewarded.

Figure 39B shows how poor overhead tactics can be defeated by a determined defense. This point begins the same way with a deep lob return by receiver M. Server B plays his overhead down the line past modified net man N, but not very deep. Furthermore, player B "telegraphs" the direction of his overhead so that alert receiver M has time to anticipate, call "Mine," and race along the base line in back of player N to retrieve the ball. Player M lobs the ball deep and returns to his side of the court. Player B again reveals the direction of his overhead and again hits the ball shallow. This allows player M to play a great low, top-spin backhand cross court which forces player B to volley up. Modified net man N foresees the cross-court return, poaches sharply to his left to intercept the ball, and gains a surprise winner.

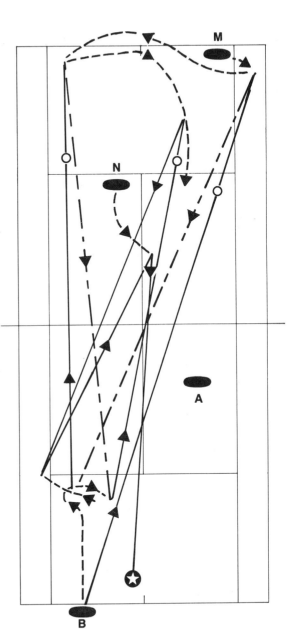

Figure 40

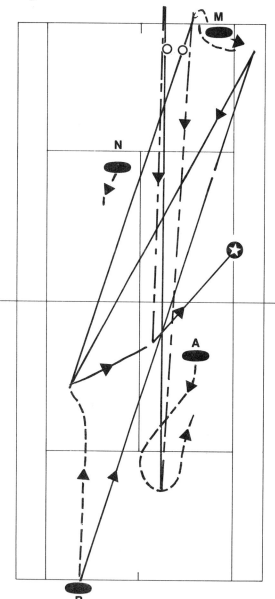

OVERHEAD PLAY

Figure 40A illustrates good
overhead-play teamwork.
Receiver M's return of service is
volleyed deep to the base line,
which causes player M to elect to
hit a deep lob. Net man A drops
way back to play a safe overhead
deep to the middle. The return
lob from player M is short.
Player B senses this and also
notes his partner has not yet
recovered position following his
overhead. Therefore, he yells
"Mine," poaches rapidly into his
partner's court, and blocks away
a spectacular winner.

Figure 40B is another example of team play. After playing his first volley to the center, server B is drawn wide by a soft angle volley stroked by receiver M. Player B replies with a sharply angled cross-court volley. He expects still another cross-court volley to be hit up by player M, so he moves toward the net for the kill. However, M crosses him up by hitting a cross-court lob volley out of reach. Fortunately, net man A detects this instantaneously, races back, turns, notes the positions of the opponents, and blocks a backhand overhead deep down the middle for a fine placement.

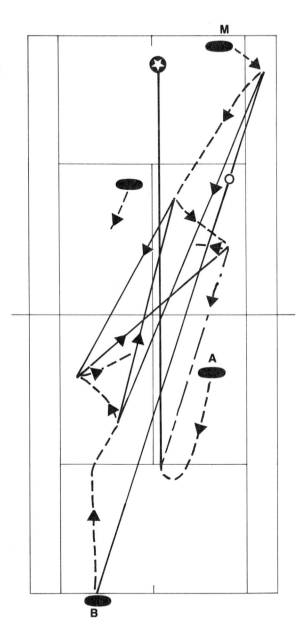

passed at net and have to lunge for the ball, a soft volley is often a wise return, as it keeps the ball low and slows the pace sufficiently to allow the volleyer time to regain his position. Examples of tactical uses of the soft volley are shown in Figure 41.

The drop volley is used to try to gain a placement when the opponents are out of position. To be successful, it requires the proper combination of touch and deception. It is not an easy shot to play, and is not recommended for the novice. The perfect drop volley is tennis artistry of the highest order. It demands delicate touch, with the wrist breaking on impact (instead of punching forward) to allow the open racket head to rebound backward, taking all of the force out of the shot so that it drops dead in the opponents' court.

On soft, slow courts the drop volley can be devastating. But a less than perfect drop volley, particularly on fast courts, practically gives the point away, as one of the opponents should bang it away wearing a big smile.

Examples of the drop volley are presented in Figure 42.

The Lob Volley

No stroke in tennis is more beautiful to behold, or more satisfying for the inveterate doubles player to play, than a lob-volley placement. It is a shot which is seldom utilized unless your team is in difficulty, which is all the more reason to be elated when the shot is successful. It is the same feeling one gets from holing out from a deep sand trap!

To be completely successful, the shot has to have several attributes. First, it should catch the opponents by surprise and, hopefully, off balance or moving in the wrong direction. Second, it cannot be too low, or it will become an easy sitter to be knocked down your throat by a devastating overhead. And, third, it cannot be too high or it can be retrieved by the opposition. In other words, it has to thread the needle by floating majestically over the heads of dismayed and stunned opponents along a beautiful parabola to a wide-open spot near the base line. Only about one percent of doubles placements are won with this delicate shot, but the thrill makes each one long remembered.

Figure 43 illustrates use of the lob volley.

Ground Strokes at Net

During net play a short volley or ground stroke by the opponents often produces a bounding ball in the forecourt. The tactics for handling such situations are largely dictated by the height of the bounce.

If the bounding ball reaches the height of the net or higher, it is best to concentrate on winning the point outright. You should be able to spot many holes in the defense through which you can drive hard, flat or top-spin placements at point-blank range. In order to avoid the embarrassment of having your shot intercepted by a scrambling opponent, you must survey the scene at the last moment before striking the ball. If the ball takes a high bounce, most players elect to employ an overhead to achieve maximum power. And on an intermediate bounce many players crouch somewhat to permit an overhead stroke.

On the other hand, a low-bouncing ball seldom opens up a placement opportunity. The best weapons to employ in this situation are dink or spin shots at the feet or wide of the opponents to force them to hit up.

Typical plays involving forecourt ground strokes are shown in Figure 44.

The Poach

The poach is an important aspect of doubles. It entails a violation of your partner's rights in that the act of poaching consists of invading his territorial domain to play a shot directed toward him. It follows rather obviously that unsuccessful poaching places a real strain on teamwork (and sometimes on marriage). On the other hand, successful poaching can change the outcome of a match because of the unsettling effect it has on the opponents. Therefore, it is important to understand the tactics of poaching.

The first rule is not to invade your partner's court unless the move is judged to produce a more effective shot. In fact, the shot should have about a two-to-one chance of resulting in a kill; otherwise, the poach presents an advantage to the enemy, as it leaves your team out of position. A study of ace poachers did indeed show they won twice as many points as they lost. They did best on weak returns of first serves, achieving a four-to-one win ratio.

To become an expert poacher a player must have excellent anticipation and timing. It also helps to bring along speed, agility, a long reach, and an ability to kill the volley. The trick is to study the striker's stroke-production methods, wait until he is fully committed to the anticipated shot, take off quickly to make the expected interception (with the long reach correcting for most miscalculations), and volley forcefully.

Figure 41

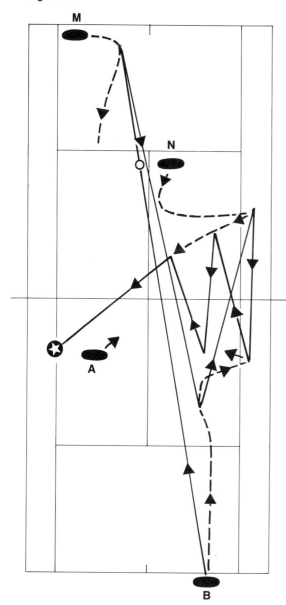

THE SOFT VOLLEY

Figure 41A illustrates great modified-net play. Receiver M plays an effective return of service which forces server B to volley up. Modified net player N senses this and starts to cut off the normally cross-court volley over the low portion of the net. Player B notes this move and tries to win the point outright by changing direction and steering his first volley down the line. Player N is forced to reverse, lunge for the ball, and is barely able to play a soft volley down the alley. Server B closes in and hits a volley toward the opening created, only to find player N has scrambled back to close the gap. In fact, player N is able to return another soft volley, this time at the feet of player B, forcing him to volley up. Keyed up and expecting a kill, player N moves in to cut off the return with a firm angle volley for a placement.

Figure 41B shows how receiver M extricates herself from a poor defensive position with a soft volley and turns the tide in her favor. Server B makes a fine first volley at the feet of receiver M and moves in close to net expecting an easy win. Receiver M quickly notes the danger and decides the only hope is to hit a soft volley just over the net and wide. This shot selection forces server B to veer to her left to dig the volley out of the ground. Player M correctly anticipates B's return must be played cross court, dashes to her left, and is rewarded with a deep volley down the line for a great win.

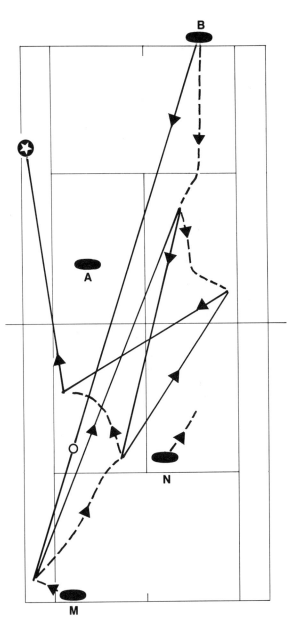

Figure 42

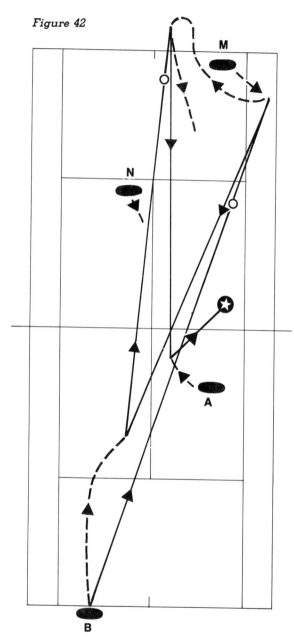

THE DROP VOLLEY

Figure 42A represents a classic drop-volley sequence. Server B follows his serve in to net and volleys the return of service deep in the court to hold receiver M on the base line. Player M returns a ground stroke down the middle which net man A decides to cut off when he realizes the whole service court is open and literally beckoning for a drop volley. As shown, this obvious tactical choice results in an easy winner.

Figure 42B shows how a slightly errant drop shot can result in disaster. Receiver M has made an excellent dink-shot return of service which server B can barely reach after a long run. Player B sees modified net man N start to his right to cover the expected cross-court volley over the low part of the net. As a result, player B decides to counter this move by dumping a drop volley into the open court straight ahead. Unfortunately, the drop volley is a bit deep, so that player N can reverse direction and dash to net to return the ball. He has a multiple choice of driving down the line or lobbing cross court for the point.

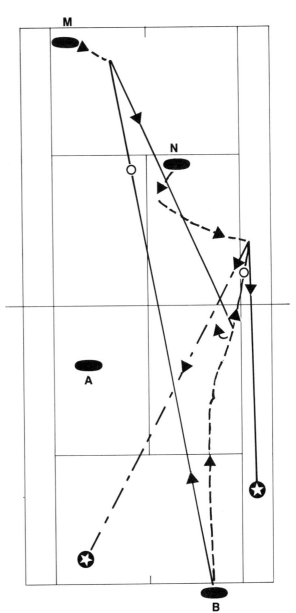

Figure 43

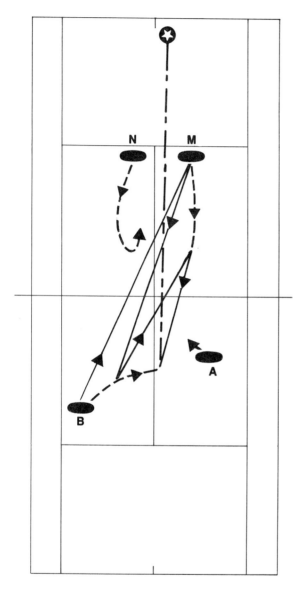

THE LOB VOLLEY

Figure 43A begins with server B hitting his first volley to receiver M, who has followed his return of service in to net. Receiver M and server B begin an exchange of soft volleys at each other's feet. Player M believes he is getting the better of the duel and moves in close to the net, along with partner N in expectation of a kill. Player B senses he is in deep trouble, as the opponents are almost on top of him. In unbelievably rapid sequence player B anticipates player M's volley toward his partner's court, reasons he is in the better position to make the return, and elects to poach. At the very last moment he decides to lob-volley. This results in an unexpected but lovely placement as players M and N are caught by surprise and moving in the wrong direction. Cheers from the gallery are in order.

Figure 43B shows the lob volley as a vehicle for taking advantage of poor team positioning. Receiver M plays an excellent return of serve which server B is barely able to hit up with a feeble cross-court return. Both player B and his partner, net man A, decide the reply will be aimed down the open middle. As a result they both move fast to cover the center. Player M notes that both his opponents are over-committed and elects to surprise them by lofting an arching lob volley over the outstretched rackets of A and B for a heady win.

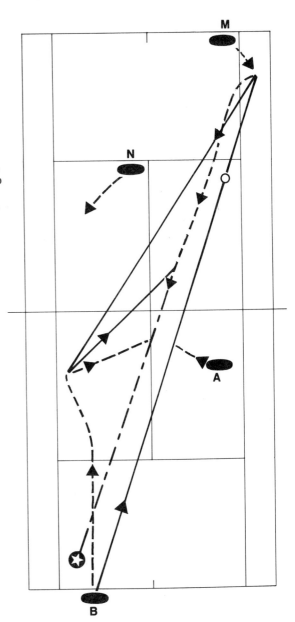

Figure 44

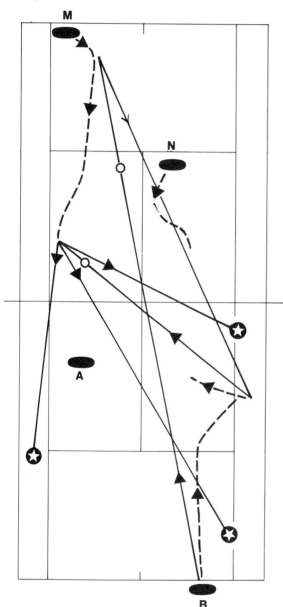

FORECOURT GROUND STROKES

Figure 44A illustrates the many possibilities open to receiver M after his excellent return of service has forced server B to volley up cross court. The volley lands near the net and bounces up to net height. Player M has time to run in to net, survey the positions of his opponents, and hit the ball through any one of the three openings shown, and perhaps others.

Figure 44B indicates how drastically the situation can change even though the point begins with the same serve and return of service. However, this time server B hits a first volley with spin to keep the bounce low. With net man A holding his ground to prevent player M from hitting down the line, player B senses that player M will hit a soft cross-court return. Once the position of M's body and racket confirms this reasoning, player B storms in toward the net and cuts the ground stroke off for a fine winner.

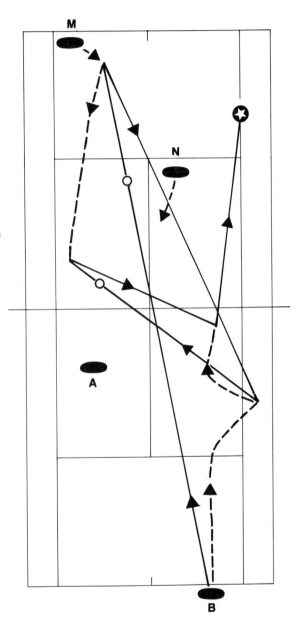

Figure 45

THE POACH

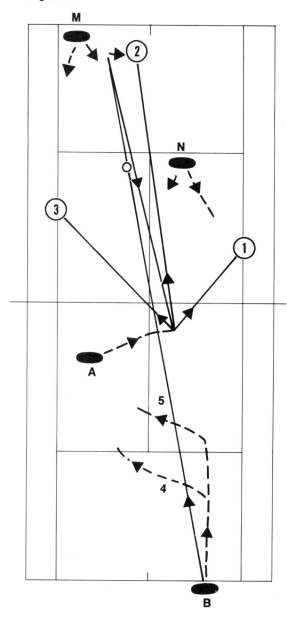

Figure 45A shows doubles' most commonly used poach. It is made by net player A after a strong first serve has forced a weak cross-court return of service.

Net man A can make such poaches on his own or using the signaled poach. In either case his play is the same. He holds his ground while anticipating receiver M's return until M is fully committed. Then he makes his fast dash cross court to volley toward one of the aim points shown, depending on the defensive positions of the opposing team. He should try for a placement, as his team may not be in position to handle a reply.

Server B approaches the net in the usual way and then crosses over to the unprotected court along path 5 for an unsignaled poach. On a signaled poach server B starts up the same path to avoid tipping off receiver M, and then veers left along path 4 to protect the left side.

Figure 45B shows the defense against the poach. The defense of aim point 1 is the responsibility of modified net man N. If he watches net man A as receiver M is about to play the return of service, he has a fairly good chance of moving to the right spot to intercept the ball and volley a winner down the open alley to area 6.

The defense of area 2 is best left to receiver M because he has more time and less chance for error than player N.

It is not easy for net man A to volley to aim point 3, as he has to reach out ahead of the ball. If, however, the shot is played, it is the responsibility of receiver M to cover the area. If he can get a quick start and reach the ball, he may be rewarded with a winner down the empty sideline to area 7.

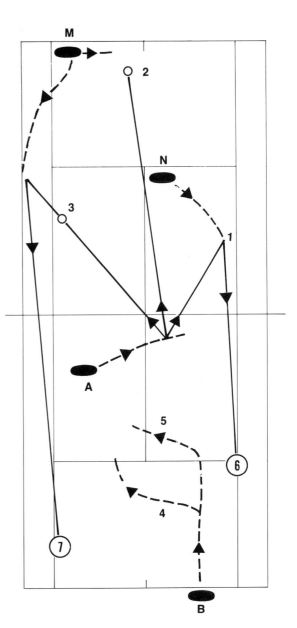

Figure 46

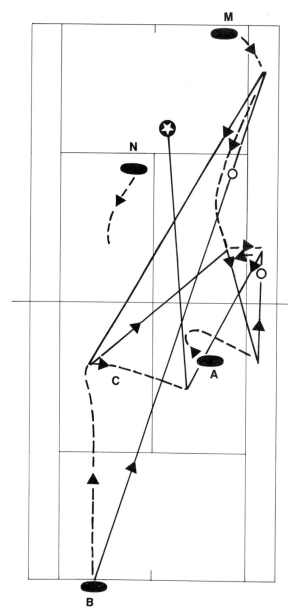

M

N

C

A

B

A FANTASTIC DEFENSIVE POACH

This point illustrates the never-say-die attitude of championship teams in a finals.

Receiver M plays a soft dink cross-court return and follows his shot rapidly to the net. Server B's first volley is a soft angle shot. As he watches this, net man A guesses that player M will reply with another soft cross-court volley and moves to cut it off. But player M glimpses this, changes intentions, and dumps a volley into the alley. This forces player A to jam on the brakes, reverse direction, make a frantic dash, and dive for the volley. He just manages to hit up a weak shot which bounces on the other side of the net, and then skids flat on his stomach. Player M observes player A trying unsuccessfully to arise, takes careful aim, and hits an apparent winner into the open court. But wait. Server B has also been observing the scene. He edges toward the action and pauses at point C to hide his intentions until he is sure player M is committed. Then he poaches like a rocket into the unmanned righthand court and produces a spectacular volley save. His still prostrate partner joined in the applause. After all, it is not very courteous under these circumstances to accuse your partner of hogging the court!

In net play the poach may assume either an offensive or a defensive role. The offensive poach, or poach of opportunity, covers all those cases in which a player moves into his partner's territory after instant judgment leads him to the belief he stands a better chance of making a placement or a strong forcing shot than does his partner. This could result from his being nearer the net, having a better angle for the shot, noting his partner is slightly out of position, or deciding a stronger forehand would offer an advantage over a backhand. The defensive poach is a point-saving maneuver which is used when one's partner is hopelessly out of position. The play usually involves a strategic delay—waiting until the last second to draw a shot toward the uncovered area and then dashing to the anticipated aim point.

As a tactic the poach can be very unnerving to the opposition for several reasons. First, it can turn what started out to be a good, well-placed shot by your team into an easy point for the poacher. Second, it forces the striker to be wary of the positions of the other team up to the last moment before concentrating on the ball as he produces his shot. This can lead to errors. And, third, it sometimes causes the striker to use too large a margin of safety in avoiding the potential poacher, which can result in poor tactics or errors.

To make poaching on the serve most effective, a set of signals should be worked out, as was noted in Figure 13. A fake poach is often very helpful when serving a crucial point, such as advantage out. Whether the poach is fake or not, the server must follow the flight of the ball carefully, as he has to cover shots which sail past the poacher.

A note of warning: Poaching can be overdone. Being a court-hog is not sound doubles tactics.

Figures 45 and 46 illustrate both typical and fantastic poaching sequences (see pages 146 to 148).

The Drift

A smart variation of the poach, which the authors have christened the "drift," has been made popular by the Australians. The drift has two variants, one for the serving team and one for the receiving team.

The serving-team drift is a maneuver initiated by net player A, who, upon anticipating a cross-court return of service by receiver M, moves, slides, or drifts along the net position toward the middle of the court (see Figure 47). This tactic produces several advantages: (1) it permits the server to come up wide to cover sharp angles, presenting a blanket

Figure 47

THE SERVING TEAM DRIFT

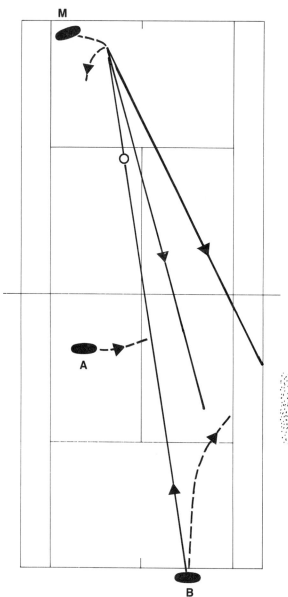

Since most returns of serve are hit cross court, net player A slides or drifts toward the middle of the court to cut down the area of safe return by receiver M, while server B comes up wide to protect against the sharply angled return. This tactic puts pressure on the receiver and results in a lot óf errors hit into area E. The defense against this formation is an occasional return down the line to keep net player A honest.

Figure 48

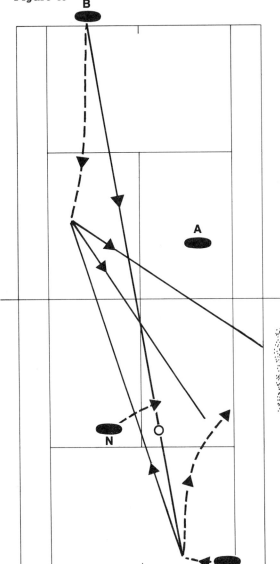

THE RECEIVING TEAM DRIFT

Since most first volleys are aimed cross court over the low portion of the net, modified net player N slides or drifts to the middle of the court to cut down the area of safe volley for server B, while receiver M comes up wide to cover angled volleys. This tactic tends to unnerve the server and results in a number of errors landing in area E. The antidote for server B is to drop an occasional volley down the line behind player N.

Figure 49

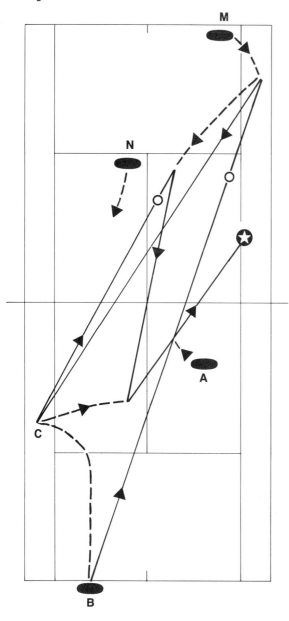

THE DRAW PLAY

Figure 49A shows a clever deliberate draw play. Receiver M has made an excellent return of service which forced server B to volley up a high-bouncing ball which lands short. Player B decides receiver M can win the point easily by hitting a forehand drive either down the middle or behind player B if she starts running toward the middle. Therefore, she elects to wait at point C to draw a shot down the middle by player M. At the moment M is committed, player B pulls a big surprise by sprinting to cut off the ball and turn a point almost certainly lost into a great placement.

Figure 49B illustrates an almost unbelievable desperation draw play which occurred in a championship final. We begin play with server B hitting a sharply angled first volley which almost won the point. After a long run receiver M barely reaches the ball and tries to slip it down the alley. But net man A diagnoses this and is able to play a sharply angled cross-court volley. This is anticipated by modified net player N and he is able to retrieve the ball and attempt to play it through the middle. Server B has expected that return and is prepared to punch one down the middle to end the point. Player M, on his way back toward the middle, recognizes the situation is almost hopeless. He decides to pause at point C until player B is about to hit, and then sprints to cut off the volley to produce a heart-stopping placement.

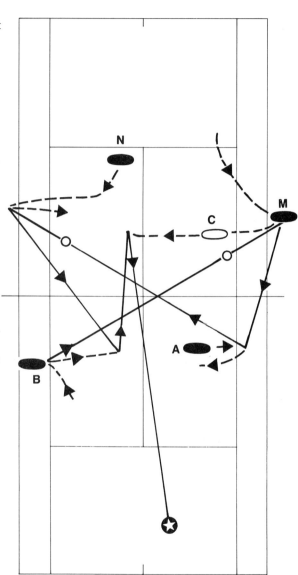

defense with two players in position to cover that half of the court toward which the ball is being struck; (2) it provides the net player easier access to volley away returns of service down the middle; (3) it opens the door for the net player to continue his drift into a poach if the return of service is weak and high; and (4) it puts tremendous pressure on the receiver, forcing him to watch the position of the net man longer and more carefully, while also restricting him to a much smaller target area for an effective return of service. Without doubt, the drift will precipitate above-normal return-of-service errors.

The receiving-team drift is a maneuver initiated by the modified net player as the server gets set to make his first volley. As soon as player N detects that server B's first volley will be played cross court or hit up, he moves across the center line toward the net (see Figure 48 on page 151). This tactic provides these advantages: (1) it permits the modified net player to volley away many weak first volleys by server B; (2) it engineers a better defense because receiver M can come up wide to cover the sharply angled volley; and (3) by forcing server B to thread the needle with his first volley, it often pressures him into making errors.

The basic concept behind the two drift tactics is directed at taking advantage of the fact that the overwhelming majority of returns of service and first volleys are hit cross court. Exploitation of such percentage odds usually results in winners far exceeding the losers. If the opponents start to defend against this by hitting down the line, various fake drift movements will be introduced and a whole new tactical battle will emerge. Thus the infinite variety of tennis.

The Draw Play

The tactic we have named the "draw play" represents really superior net-play teamwork. It consists of a complex maneuver during which the team at a tactical disadvantage purposely entices the opponents into hitting a "sure winner" toward an artificial or contrived opening, only to close the gap at the last moment and fashion a winner.

There are two versions of the draw—one in which you deliberately move or remain out of position to invite an opening, the other in which your team has been forced so far out of position that a complete recovery before the opponent's next shot is impossible. The most common example of the "deliberate" draw play is a fake poach by the net man, who starts his poach too soon in order to draw a return of service down the sideline, then reverses quickly to volley deep cross court for the point. The situation is much more complex when your team has been forced far out of position. To pull off a "desperation" draw play you have an instant—the one right instant—to start running to cut off the return hit into the gap. If you start too late, you will be unable to reach the ball; and if you start too soon, the opponents can change their shot and hit the ball behind you for an easy win. The time for decision is mighty short, but the reward for the proper answer is great: it can turn a point that has been hopelessly lost into a sensational winner.

Figure 49 explains draw-play tactics (see pages 152 to 153).

7

BASE-LINE PLAY

This chapter considers base-line play other than the serve and return of service, which have already been covered in earlier text.

In top-flight singles the importance of base-line play in winning points varies tremendously, depending upon the types of games the opponents elect to employ, and the playing speed of the particular court surface. This makes it impossible to generalize on base-line tactics, which adds greatly to the fascination of this remarkably diverse and ever-changing game.

For example, on fast courts with two men who are serve-and-volley artists facing each other, base-line play consisting of forcing shots, passing shots, and lobs will account for about 10 to 15 percent of all winners, while net play consisting of first volleys, later volleys, overheads, and close-in ground strokes will account for about 25 to 35 percent of all winners. When a serve-and-volley expert faces a steady base-liner, the winning percentages change to equal at about 25 percent each. And when two base-line protagonists square off, the base-line shots increase in importance to win about 40 percent as against roughly 15 percent from the net shots.

The data on fast courts are somewhat different for women. The serve-and-volley opponents win about 25 to 30 percent of points from the net and an equal percentage from the base line. A serve-and-volley player matched against a base-liner will switch the winners to about 40 to 50 percent from the base line and 20 to 30 percent from the net position.

On slow courts the situation is entirely different. Not even the best of big serve-and-volley players among the men can exercise successfully the option of following serve to net and camping there. Data indicate that serve-and-volley opponents end up winning from 45 to 60 percent of points from the base-line and only 12 to 30 percent at the net, with few first-volley winners. When some of the women who specialize in base-line play perform on a slow court, the point exchanges from the base line extend for an average of about fifteen shots. And some rallies, interspersed with "moon" balls, have been known to last almost twenty minutes! In that situation you better know how to play base-line shots because they win almost 80 percent of the points!

In an important sense, the hallmark of the great singles players over history has been their ability to stroke consistently deep ground strokes from the base line. Without this skill, they could not win on slow courts, and thus would not become classified as all-court champions.

In sharp contrast, the hallmark of the great doubles players has been to desert the base line and journey to the net as soon as possible in order to avoid having to play ground strokes from the base line, irrespective of the speed of the court. That is a disaster area from which only 10 to 20 percent of doubles points are won. And the strokes required to extricate yourself from that losing zone are quite different from those ordinarily used to advantage in singles.

By now it should be obvious that tactical discussions of base-line play for singles and doubles must be treated separately.

SINGLES PLAY FROM THE BASE LINE

A clear and comprehensive description of the tactics of base-line play is an extremely difficult undertaking. Because of the almost infinite variety in the base-line game brought about by differing styles of play, likes and dislikes of opponents, and court surfaces, it is practical to present only the key points in this section. This will involve discussion of forcing shots and passing shots, including lobs.

Forcing Shots

First a few introductory comments.

When you and your opponent are both on the base line engaging in an exchange of ground strokes, you must remember that such rallies are fencing operations. You have to "move the opponent around" by one means or another in order to try to extract an error or a weak return, or to create an opening. Moving the other player around may mean running him from side to side, or up and back, or changing direction, speed, or spin, or "wrong-footing" him by hitting behind him as he moves in the wrong direction. Whatever method you use, once you engineer an opening, be prepared to take advantage of the opportunity by hitting the correct forcing shot. Otherwise, your opponent will recover the proper ready position and you will have wasted the advantage you just worked so hard to gain.

The second thing to remember is to hit the ball within your capabilities. Whamming the ball may win a few spectacular points, but it usually leads to more spectacular errors. Keeping the ball under control and in play leads to victory over many an opponent.

The third item should now be a familiar requirement: you should work on anticipation. Otherwise, you will not be able to cover the wide expanse of court. Generally, you should start from the ready position at the middle of, and about a foot back of, the base line and return promptly to that point between strokes. Study of your opponent's stroke-production techniques should permit you to move in the right direction and avoid being "wrong-footed." All those players who appear to play the game "effortlessly" have captured the art of anticipation.

And, finally, in striving to improve your base-line play, practice keeping the ball deep. That is the trademark of the accomplished player. Deep shots can be hit safely two or three feet above the net—you should avoid netting the ball. Your opponent can seldom make a truly offensive return from deep court, and is deprived of the drop-shot return option (unless you have a broken leg).

Now let us consider the three types of forcing shots:

1. Sheer Power Type

Some players just hit the ball so hard to the corners of the base line that they can run the opposing player out of position and draw weak returns or create openings which lead to winners. They always capitalize on short returns (landing more than ten feet inside the base line) by playing the forcing approach shot and taking the net to volley any return. These should be kept low to prevent effective lobbing by the opponent. This tactic, properly applied, should win almost 90 percent of the time. Examples of typical points are shown in Figures 50, 51, and 52.

Figure 50

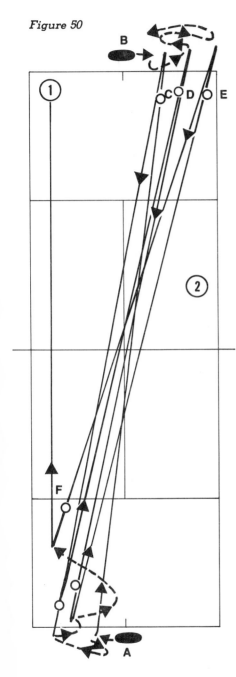

CLASSICAL FORCING SHOTS

Shown here is a classical sequence of forcing shots from the backhand side used by some of the great clay-court players. As earlier mentioned, clay-court points can go on for minutes, and trying to follow a diagram of one would strain both the reader's eyes and patience. Therefore, this diagram begins just a few strokes from the finish. Player A exchanges three deep backhand returns with player B to points C, D, and E, driving him farther to his left each time. Note that both players return to the ready position to permit complete court coverage. Finally, when player B is forced wide of the court to return the ball landing at point E, he makes a short return to point F. This opens up the court for player A to crack a hard backhand down the line which player B would need a bicycle to reach. If player B had anticipated the shot and was indeed pedaling fast down the base line, player A could "wrong-foot" him by faking the drive and hitting a soft, sharply angled shot behind him to aim point 2 for the win.

Figure 51

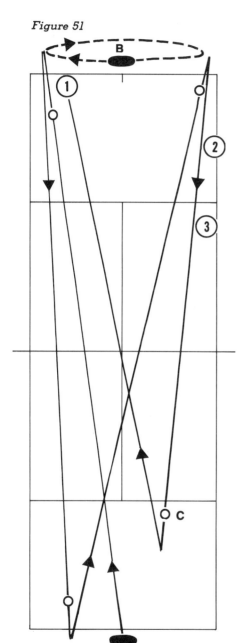

FORCING CORNER TO CORNER

Another favorite tactic is the murderous sequence of forcing your opponent to run back and forth from corner to corner until you drive him out of position. Once again the diagram begins just a few strokes before the winning shot. Player A directs a forehand cross court to the sideline, and blasts the return cross court to the backhand corner. This runs player B wide and draws a shallow return to point C. From this commanding forecourt position player A has three choices for a win. He can hit another hard cross-court to the open corner at aim point 1. If player B is running hard to cover that shot, player A can drive the ball behind him to aim point 2, or slice the ball short and wide to aim point 3.

Figure 52

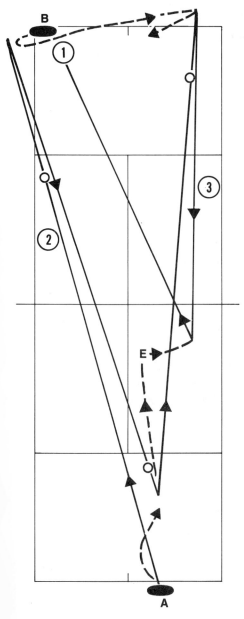

FOLLOWING A FORCING SHOT TO NET

Server A's wide serve to the forehand has pulled player B off the court and drawn a short return to the middle. The proper tactic is to waste no time in hitting the forcing shot down the line and taking the net. As pointed out in Figure 25, the down-the-line shot provides you the shortest route to the proper volleying position, point E slightly on the down-the-line side of the center service line. From this position player A can cover the attempted fast down-the-line passing shot and volley an easy winner to the open court at aim point 1. Also open for consideration are a sharply angled volley to aim point 2 or a soft volley to aim point 3 if player B is committed to trying to cover the cross-court volley.

Certain players develop excellent cross-court and down-the-line passing shots from the deep corner. Against such players it is often better to hit the forcing approach shot to the center to cut down the angle available for the return.

2. Tactical Type

Most players are not equipped with overwhelming power, so they have to resort to trying to out-think and out-maneuver the opponent. Usually, this entails trying to find a weakness in the opponent's game which you can exploit wisely. This means to exploit it only to gain crucial points, because the intelligent adversary may diagnose your tactics and find a means of correcting the defect in his armor.

The control of the ball which can be achieved by the top players is uncanny. We know of a match involving a craftsman against a player having a better backhand than a forehand. The result was that the latter player cannot remember having the opportunity to play a single backhand in a three-set match! In another encounter at Davis Cup level, one contestant tested a rumored low, running, backhand weakness of his opponent on the very first point and extracted an error. He walked past one of the authors sitting on the sideline and whispered that the match was over. And it was—in three straight sets.

In weekend play weaknesses are more prevalent, so that tactical choices can often be broader. If your opponent likes to slug, feed him soft shots and spin which dampens the pace of his returns. If your opponent likes to come to net and you have trouble passing him, try lobbing. The lobs do not have to be low offensive lobs. Safe, high lobs are difficult to hit, as the ball drops down almost vertically. If your opponent hates to volley, draw him forward and pass or lob him. If she employs top-spin ground strokes, deliver low, spinning shots. And if she is slow of foot, try some drop shots. Keep probing until you find the chinks in her armor.

Typical tactical forcing shots are shown in Figures 53 and 54.

3. Continuous-Pressure Type

In a sense, the important tactic of getting each ball back as deep as prudent risk permits is a form of forcing game. Such pressure often goads an opponent into becoming more and more impatient. This invites errors either through attempting shots too difficult to produce, or overhitting. Many a big hitter has blown up under this sort of subtle pressure.

Passing Shots

In order to break serve and win matches against the player who employs the volley well, you must have in your arsenal of weapons some effective passing shots.

To acquire expertise in knowing when to try to pass, you must understand the odds for success you face from various court positions. It stands to reason that your chances of winning depend in large measure on how far away you are from the net (roughly representing the relative distance away from the opposing volleyer) at the moment you stroke the ball. When balls driven by your opponent land within about ten feet of your base line, your chances of passing a good volleyer are almost nil. However, on balls landing ten to eighteen feet (the service line) short of the base line, the odds shift in favor of the passer and he should be able to win about two out of three opportunities. On balls landing inside the service line, the volleyer becomes a sitting duck—the passer should win about seven out of eight attempts.

The importance to the passer of the short ball cannot be overemphasized. The players should understand that short-ball opportunities are in the minority and such golden chances must not be wasted. An important factor in capitalizing on the short ball is anticipating when to expect it and where it may land in order to get set for the shot. Typical situations which provide advance warning are:

1. A return of service which forces the net-rushing server to volley up from near the service line T is likely to land short near the center.

2. A return which forces the volleyer to reach far to one side will usually be popped up down the line.

3. A return which the net player must half-volley will ordinarily have little pace, and the direction can be diagnosed.

4. A cross-court dink return which the net player must volley up will usually be hit cross-court over the lowest portion of the net.

Diagrams of passing shot plays are shown in Figures 55 and 56.

And, finally, do not underestimate the value of the lob. We have already noted in Figure 26 the use of the offensive lob. The high defensive lob is also a good method of dislodging the net player. Few weekend players have consistent overheads, so that you can win many a point by tossing up a high lob from a seemingly hopeless court position. Remember that sometimes the sun and wind, and always the opponent's errors, will supplement your stroke-production capabilities. Even if your opponent does smash the ball back, at least you will have had

Figure 53

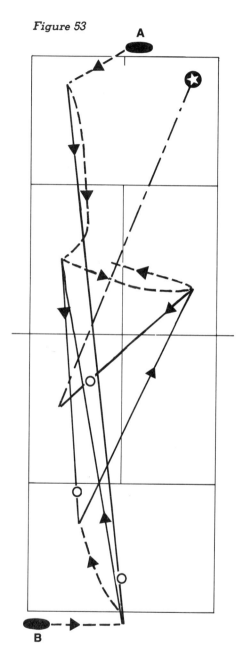

TACTICAL FORCING SHOTS

This point illustrates how a fine selection of shots can win for the defender. We pick up the point as server A takes the net on a ground stroke hit deep to the middle. Receiver B notes this and hits a soft top-spin forehand cross court which forces player A to volley up short. Player B moves in and elects to hit a cross-court dink which forces the volleyer to stretch. Player B anticipates a cross-court answering angled volley, so he moves forward. As he reaches the ball he fakes a down-the-line return to entice player A into running full speed toward the sideline. At the last moment he tosses up a beautiful backhand offensive lob cross court to the corner, which his opponent can only stare at in both shock and admiration.

Figure 54

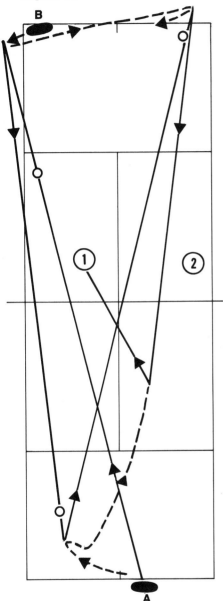

THE DROP SHOT

This diagram shows the correct employment of the drop shot. Server A draws receiver B off the court with a sliced serve and then plays a strong cross-court forcing shot off the return of service. Player B barely gets to the ball and makes a weak return within the service court. Player A notes that B is back at the ready position expecting another forcing shot, so he fakes one and then catches player B by surprise by dumping a little drop shot to aim point 1 or 2. This is a shot which usually cannot be made from deep in the court, as it gives the opponent time to retrieve the ball, and often gives away the point. Drop shots are especially effective in women's singles, as their court-covering capability is less.

Figure 55

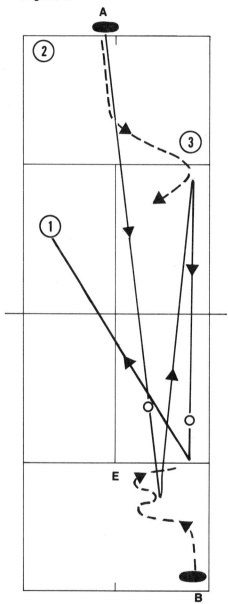

CLASSICAL PASSING TACTICS

This diagram illustrates classical passing opportunities initiated by a forcing return of service delivered by receiver B. Player B runs around a shallow serve and plays a forehand down the line. He anticipates server A will have to volley up, so he pauses at E in expectation. When the volley lands short he moves over quickly for an easy cross-court passing shot to aim point 1 or 2. Should server A be moving rapidly to cover the cross-court return, player B can slip the ball down the sideline behind him to aim point 3.

Figure 56

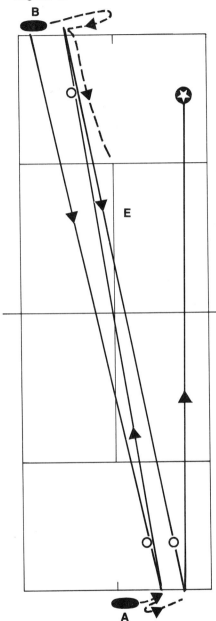

PASSING AFTER TACTICAL ERRORS

We enter into a long base-line exchange near its conclusion. Player B hits a deep cross-court drive which player A returns deep cross court. Player B becomes impatient and makes two tactical errors. First, he decides to try to end the point by going to net from the base line instead of waiting for a short ball. And, second, he goes to net behind a cross-court shot, which means he has to run all the way to point E to be in position to cover the down-the-line passing shot. Player A knows all of this and can hardly believe it when he sees player B start for the net. He moves quickly into position to take advantage of the opening and drills a winning forehand passing shot down the line. The brain flashed the signal to select the down-the-line shot so fast that player A hardly realized he was indeed "thinking while playing."

Figure 57

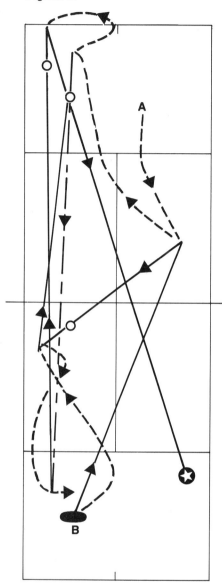

HIGH DEFENSIVE LOB

This point illustrates great defensive play employing the high lob. We join the long point as player A is approaching the net and player B elects to hit a dink to the feet to force a short volley. As he sees this tactic succeeding, player B moves in and hits what he thinks is a winner down the line. However, player A has read his intentions and initiates a breakneck-speed retreat toward the base line. He is barely able to reach the ball, and the only shot he can elect is to hit up a high defensive lob to give himself time to reorganize. Player B senses what is about to happen and retreats to get set for an overhead. He circles to play it from the forehand side and smashes one into the corner. Once again player B thinks the point is over and stands to admire his shot. But player A has recovered position in the middle of the base line, is able to retrieve the ball, and makes a great cross-court drive for the win. One moral is never give up the ship, and the other is never pause to admire your shot, no matter how beautiful.

time to get back into position to attempt to return the ball. Never give up the ship (see Figure 57)!

DOUBLES PLAY FROM THE BASE LINE

The one objective of doubles play from the base line is to extricate yourself from that plague-ridden area using approach shots which will permit you a safe journey to the far more advantageous net position.

Since the team at net has the offensive position, it is not easy for the player pinned in the back court to maneuver his team into net position. This requires sound thinking as well as sound stroke production. Perseverance, even in the most helpless situations, is often rewarded. Remember, your opponents will make more errors than placements. Even the great champions have overhit simple sitters through eagerness brought on by the thrill of the impending kill.

The proper team formation for base-line play depends, of course, upon the circumstances. The best position for receiving service is with the receiver's partner at the modified net position, as already described in Figure 8. In most cases he should strive to move to and hold the most advantageous net position, so this leaves the receiving team with a one-up, one-back formation if the receiver cannot follow his return of service in to net. If the modified net player is forced to retreat, the players should normally adopt a parallel formation with each standing about a foot behind the base line at the midpoint of his half of the court. They move from this position after anticipation of the depth and direction of the opponent's shot. When an opportunity to dash to the net is gained, they should move in together in parallel.

The strokes used in trying to approach the net—the dink, the drive, and the lob—will now be reviewed.

The Dink

The dink-shot family, including the soft top-spin shot as well as the under-spin chopped or sliced shots, is notably effective from the back court in doubles.

First, it should be made clear that there are two circumstances under which the dink should be avoided as being too dangerous: (1) when opponents are crowding the net so tightly that they might angle-volley for a placement, and (2) when you have to play the shot from so far back in the court that the opponents have sufficient time to anticipate and dash forward for the kill.

Played from ten feet or more inside the base line, the dink offers the following advantages:

1. The slow speed of the ball permits the striker time to follow in to net behind the shot.
2. The low-over-the-net, spinning nature of the shot usually forces the opponents to volley up, which gives the striker an opportunity to volley the return.
3. The soft nature of the stroke makes it easy to control and also prevents the opponents from getting much pace on the return volley.

Examples of use of the dink to gain the net are shown in Figures 58 and 59.

The Drive

Employed wisely and well, the drive can be an effective weapon from the back court. First, however, the reader should understand some of the dangers involved, such as: (1) The types of drives which must be employed in almost every case are low, flat, or sinking top-spin varieties. The high-over-the-net deep drives so valuable in many aspects of singles play are eaten alive when two opponents blanket the net. (2) For similar reasons, even a low, hard drive from near the base line is a foolish shot (unless a big hole exists), as an alert net team has plenty of time to murder such returns. (3) When in a one-up, one-back position the base-line player must avoid a drive down the line, as it gives the net player the simplest of cross-court volleys to the open diagonal (see Figure 62) for a placement.

Assuming the reader is now aware of the dangers, the drive can be very useful in the following situations:

1. It can bore a hole through the center of the opposing net team if they are positioned a step too far apart (see Figure 8 for correct position), or if they pull an Alphonse-and-Gaston act and let the ball advance too far before either player moves to stroke the ball.
2. If the opposing net team is crowding the center too much, a top-spin cross-court drive to the alley can produce a placement.
3. If the ball is played from a wide angle and the net team has not

Figure 58

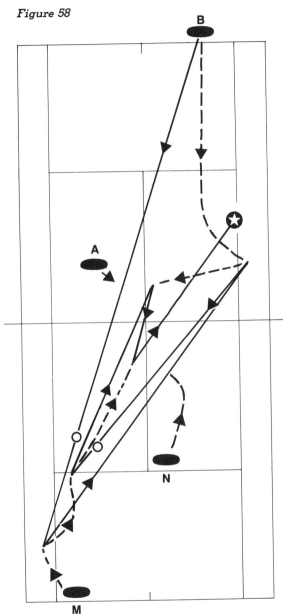

THE DOUBLE DINK APPROACH

The diagram shows a wide-angled backhand dink return of service by receiver M which server B volleys short to the service-line area. Player M moves in and plays a second dink low over the center of the net, and he and his partner edge forward to blanket the center. Server B is trapped, as he cannot do anything but hit the volley up into the face of the enemy. Receiver M has only to take two steps and end the agony with a beautiful angle volley.

Figure 59

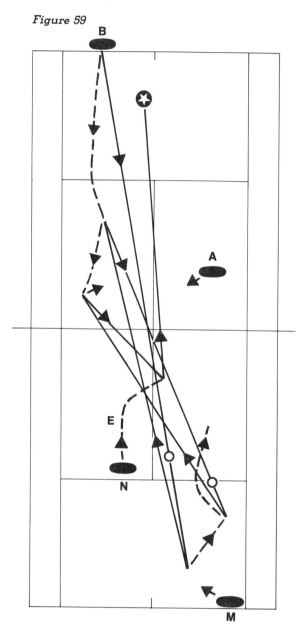

THE DINK APPROACH SHOT

This play shows a recommended low return of service down the middle which server B volleys short just beyond the service line. Receiver M runs in and hits a great, low cross-court dink. This maneuver is noted by modified net player N, who reasons that the return will almost assuredly be volleyed up cross court over the lower part of the net. Therefore, he edges forward and pauses at position E until his observation of player B's stroking actions confirms his prediction. Then he sprints cross court to execute a beautiful volley poach for the winner. This is a very satisfying experience.

properly repositioned itself (see Figure 30), drives down the line (which may not even have to pass over the net) or sharply cross court can become winners.

4. If a short volley landing near the service line bounces fairly high, it can be driven at the net team with such speed as to elicit an error or a weak return. On lower balls, a drive at the opponent's midriff is often the best tactic for drawing weak replies.

Typical driving points are presented in Figures 60 and 61. And one to be shunned is shown in Figure 62.

The Lob

The lob is an important shot which is often under-utilized in doubles. It is the best shot to use from the back court under the following circumstances:

1. When playing from more than about ten feet inside the base line against a team with one or both players crowding the net, an offensive lob should permit you to capture the·net. Remember to hit the ball deep, as the best way to be murdered legally is to lob short and run to the net.

2. A high, defensive lob is a wise tactic when the return is played from a point very deep in the court or when the striker is maneuvered way out of position by a forcing shot. It permits your team time to regain the best position, even to the extent of allowing your partner to drop back from the net to the base line if necessary. Remember to keep the ball high, because low lobs will be put away before you can return to the proper position.

3. As a surprise shot, some expert players fake a drive and use a top-spin lob which lands deep and bounds out of reach. It is not easy to control, but is a heart-stopper when it works, leaving the volleyer muttering to himself.

Lobs should generally be aimed toward a player's backhand side, as few players have a forceful backhand overhead. In fact, some players take advantage of this by hitting a low lob which forces the net player to move a few steps to hit a high backhand volley. The lobber keeps moving forward to net position and volleys the return.

In warming up for a match, take careful note of the strength and

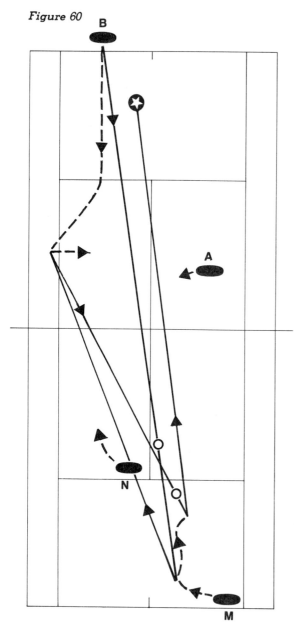

Figure 60

DRIVING THROUGH THE MIDDLE

This point presents a situation often encountered in doubles. Receiver M has played the standard cross-court return of service, and server B has replied with the standard volley near the center, but somewhat shallow. Receiver M runs forward to strike the return and notices that server B is a little slow in getting back to the basic volleying position, and that net man A has not moved enough to cover the opening in the center. Therefore, receiver M moves rapidly to drive the ball low and hard through the middle before the vulnerable gap can be closed.

Figure 61

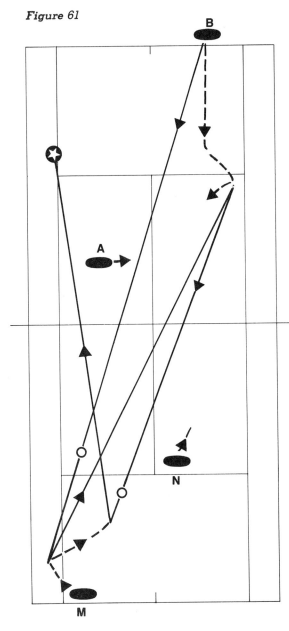

TOP-SPIN DRIVE

This particular point proved to be the match point which won a Davis Cup Challenge Round.

Receiver M hits a routine cross-court return of service which server B volleys safely down the center. At this moment net player A senses that the reply by player M will be the percentage play, which is a cross-court dink aimed at embarrassing server B. While this thinking cannot be faulted, the mistake made by player A was that he moved to the center to cut off the expected cross-court return a split second too soon. Receiver M caught this motion in his all-important peripheral vision, retained his balance and options, and was able to change directions by reaching around the ball and directing a top-spin drive down the line behind player A for a splendid win.

Figure 62

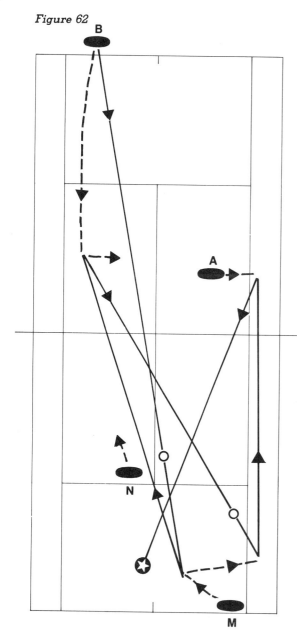

THE OPEN DIAGONAL

This particular point is representative of deplorable tactical choices, but nevertheless is often observed in weekend tennis matches. We show it here in the hope you will drop it forever from your repertoire of shots.

After server B volleys the return of service cross court, player M decides to try to slip a shot down the alley past net player A. But he forgets two things. First, this is the highest part of the net, so his drive must be high. And, second, with his partner N in the modified net position, his team is vulnerable to a simple cross-court volley into the open diagonal. That is exactly what grateful net man A executes.

The only good time to make this play is when net player A starts to poach prematurely. Even then you have to be sure he is not just trying to fool you into making the down-the-line return.

Figure 63

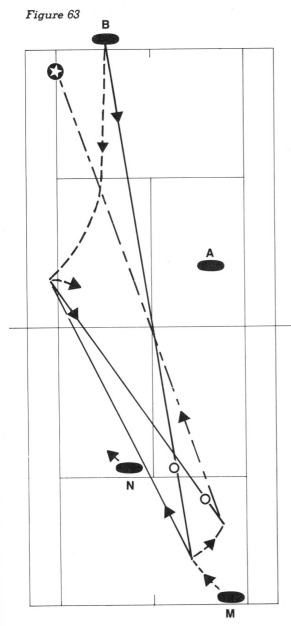

THE OFFENSIVE LOB

In this point receiver M makes
an excellent dink return of
service which forces server B to
volley cross court from close to
the net. As player M prepares to
cover the shot, he glances at
player B and notes he is still
close to the net and has left an
opening in the middle.
Therefore, player M fakes a
drive and hits a surprise
offensive lob deep to the corner
for the win.

Figure 64

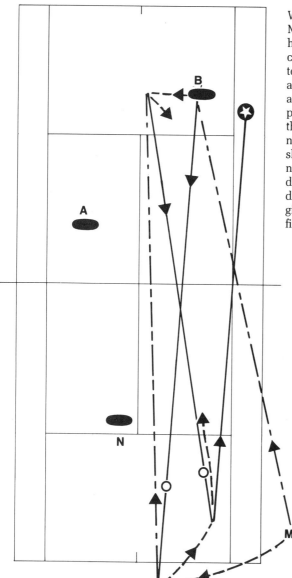

THE DEFENSIVE LOB

We enter this point with player M sending up a high lob after having been forced wide of the court. Player B smashes the lob toward the middle, and M is just able to reach the ball and toss up a high backhand lob. Player B plays another overhead toward the sideline. This time player M notes that player B has been slow in returning to the proper net position and sees an opening down the line. So player M drives one down the line, and gives credit for the win to two fine lobs.

Figure 65

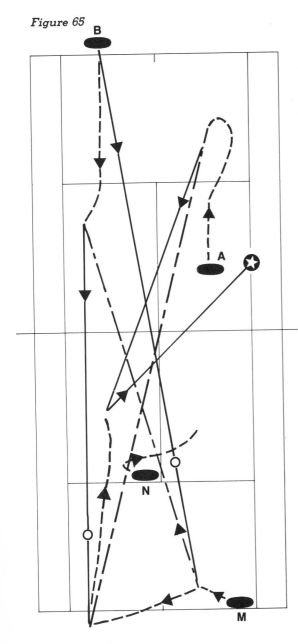

GOOD DEFENSIVE TEAM PLAY

This particular point is a great one upon which to wind up the diagrams for this book. It begins in apparent disaster, but is pulled out of the fire by brilliant team play.

Server B places an excellent fast serve into the backhand corner which almost aces receiver M. He is barely able to reach the ball and can only toss up a short defensive lob. Player M sees that server B is preparing to hit an overhead down in the direction of modified net player N. In a flash player M decides he would have a better chance to retrieve the ball, so he yells "Mine" and sets sail for the sideline while relieved player N reverses direction and moves to protect the forehand side. Player B is committed and proceeds to hit his overhead down the line. Player M makes a fantastic get and sends up a high defensive lob. As he does so, he notes it is so deep that net player A is going to have to block the overhead cross court rather than smash it forcefully. Another thought flashes through M's head, and he dashes in to net as soon as he sees player A is committed. He pulls off a beautiful backhand angled-volley winner for his second brilliant shot. That is the sort of point player M can savor for some time!

direction of the wind and sun. The height, strength, and direction of the lob may have to be altered with a change of courts between games. It is embarrassing to have a mental lapse and watch your lob be blown off court or hang in the air for an easy sitter. Remember that the wind also makes it more difficult for your opponent to hit the overhead. And there is nothing unfair about lobbing when your opponents are in the sun court.

Some typical base-line points in doubles are shown in Figures 63, 64, and 65 (see pages 177 to 179).

8

SUMMARY

The central purpose of this book is to increase the joy and satisfaction you receive from participation in the great game of tennis, whether champion, beginner, or spectator, through extending your understanding of the basic tactics of both singles and doubles. Once a player or observer starts to grasp the fundamentals of the game, he or she can begin to appreciate the complexities involved and the winning and losing strategies of the tennis contest. A key reason tennis is such a challenging sport is that the variations in player style, capabilities, and tactics on one side of the net are always matched against a different set of styles on the other side of the net, resulting in an almost unbelievable number of possible tactical situations and shot selections. This is why there is no single correct method of playing the game. And this is also why we stress that every player is always in the learning stages of understanding tennis tactics. The game is forever changing as young players with distinctive talents and new ideas emerge to duel one another. To be aware of and to appreciate fully the continuing evolution of the game of tennis and the subtleties that innovations bring to match-play maneuvers, it is essential that you first understand the fundamentals which underlie the basic tactics. Reading and rereading this book should assist in bringing added competence, enjoyment, dedication, and enthusiasm to your tennis participation.

If the suggestion sounds unrealistic or too promotional to you, just

remember that even as experienced a player and teacher as Talbert*
always reads over the summary and other pertinent portions of the earlier books before key matches in order to jog his memory and inspire
his concentration. Now he will add this book to his prematch study.

COMMON ASPECTS OF SINGLES AND DOUBLES

While singles and doubles tactics are quite diverse, the games do have
similarities. The two we would like to stress are the intellectual nature
and the speed of the games, since they dictate the importance of preparation.

Singles and doubles are both intellectual because of the essentially
infinite variety of tactical situations a player encounters in matches as a
consequence of varying conditions such as ball speed, spin, and
bounce, court surface, relative positions of players, stroke selection,
weather, etc. There is an attack for every defense and a defense for
every attack. To begin to master tactics it is essential to build up in the
brain, through playing experience, instruction, and observation, a vast
inventory of good and bad tactical choices.

Both games are fast. The travel time of the ball is very often less
than one second, so the player must continually make instantaneous
decisions.

It begins to sound like an almost impossible task for the brain to sort
out all the variables and crank out the proper tactical decision in a
fraction of a second! And it will be, unless the player makes advance
preparations.

Preparation begins with anticipation. The first step in anticipation is
the knowledge of the type of shot you have played and the range of
replies likely to be made by your opponent. Then, by studying his stroking motions, habits, and favorite shots, you can narrow the range of
possibilities and estimate the speed, spin, height, direction, and depth of
the return. Without anticipatory capabilities, your effectiveness in planning and executing appropriate returns is severely blunted.

Once you have diagnosed the type of shot being aimed in your direction, you must turn your attention to the ball and begin moving to

* William F. Talbert was ranked in the first ten in singles for thirteen years, was the
U.S. men's doubles champion four times, and mixed doubles champion four times. In
addition, he captained the U.S. Davis Cup Team to victory.

intercept the shot while planning the kind of reply you should make. Since this planning has to be accomplished almost instantaneously, your brain must be able to sense the entire situation and then communicate a command in an incredibly short time. The only way you can do this efficiently is to have developed through training and experience a storehouse of tactical knowledge. The brain can then quickly recognize the pattern of play, remember what happened before in this or other matches under similar circumstances, and crank out a shot-selection decision, or even a sequence of shot selections, leading to the winning or losing of a point. All of this information is carefully stored in the tennis-tactics inventory portion of the brain. The great players utilize that remarkable human computer to formulate correct tactical choices almost invariably. While that talent is a heavenly gift, any player can improve upon his or her shot selections through study of good players, match-play experience, reading, and practice. The object is to make the best play almost automatically.

Naturally, you have to be able to execute the desired shot to carry out the tactics. In both singles and doubles this requires combining the tactical preparation we have just described with stroke-production preparation. Together they produce the court coverage, sound footwork, balance, and fluid motions which lead to excellence in shot making. Instruction in stroke production is helpful because it is easier for others to observe flaws than for the player. You should strive for simple strokes not cluttered with unnecessary motions.

Finally, both singles and doubles are percentage games, and the percentages favor the attacker. The best attacking position is at the net. Therefore, in both games getting to net behind effective approach shots is a primary objective.

SINGLES TACTICS

If we could imprint indelibly just two words on the mind of the aspiring singles player, we would select *steadiness*, or keeping the ball in play, and *depth*. Steadiness avoids errors, which are responsible for losing from 40 to 60 percent of points, depending on whether classified as unforced or as forced-plus-unforced. And depth is the backbone of most successful attacking service, ground, and volley strokes.

The serve is the single most important stroke in modern offensive tennis. A strong serve is a must—it puts the striker on the offensive, and should of itself open the door for wins in about 40 percent of points by forcing weak returns of service or errors. The big serve is twice as effective on fast courts as on slow clay or composition courts.

The primary things to remember are to get the first serve in and to keep all serves deep. The experts accomplish both some 70 percent of the time. The real hallmark of a top server is a player who can keep the second serve deep, and away from his opponent's strength. Good first serves and good deep deliveries, whether first or second serves, ultimately produce a won point in about 75 percent of the cases.

On fast courts the top players follow every serve rapidly to the net and attempt to volley the return away for a winner. First serves are usually aimed toward the sidelines, to open up the court, and second serves at the backhand corner. On slow courts the server usually hits for the backhand corner and only occasionally follows serve in to the net position, since returns of service are more effective on such surfaces.

The return of service is probably the most difficult stroke in tennis to hit consistently. But hit it consistently you must if you are going to stand a chance of breaking your opponent's serve and winning a match. Just getting the ball back turns the odds of winning the point from two or three to one against you to about even! First, you have to learn how to position yourself for receiving the serve. There are a number of factors to consider, but, depending on the ability of the server, it is generally desirable to stand one to three feet inside the base line on a straight line drawn from the position of the server through a point in the center of the service court. On a second serve it is ordinarily best to move in another one to three feet. These receiving positions shorten the distance you have to move to one side or the other for a breaking serve, and allow you to hit the ball sooner and on the rise in order to hurry the server. Against a top server, you must also try to anticipate from his toss and actions what type of serve he will hit, in order to get a start in the right direction to reach a 100-mile-an-hour bullet.

The best aim points for a low return against a net-rushing server (Figure 15) and for a deep and higher return against a server who stays on the base line (Figure 16) should be memorized.

The net position in singles is the best attacking position only when you have prepared the way with an effective approach shot—in fact, you should keep in mind that a winning volley is really an approach-shot–volley combination. Most effectual approach shots, whether serves, returns of service, ground strokes, or lobs, are hit deep. Net play should account for 20 to 35 percent of all singles winners. To profit from the attacking net position it is important to hit the volley deep, as it is then very difficult for the opponent to pass you from the back court. On the other hand, if you volley short near the service line, you turn the odds of winning over to your opponent. You should memorize Figure 28.

When both players are on the base line, there is one overriding rule: keep the ball deep. The whole base-line game consists of fencing until you can force the opponent into hitting a ball short. This provides you with the opportunity of moving in and hitting a forcing shot, deep or angled, which you can turn into a winning point. (It is too risky to try to get in to the net from deep in the court.) Actually about seven out of eight base-line points are won after one of the players hits a short shot. The other player can then take advantage of this opening in two ways. In about two out of three cases the point is won with a forcing shot which will score a placement or elicit an error. In the third case the player can make a forcing shot, follow it in to the net, and then volley away the return for the point. During base-line rallies, assume each shot will be returned and concentrate on anticipating its direction and depth so that you can move to the proper position.

Finally, it is wise to remember the effect of court surfaces on tactics. One player put it in a nutshell this way: "Here on grass you hit the big serve, run to the net, punch that crisp volley, and the point is over. On our clay courts you can hit that big serve, run to the net, punch that crisp volley, and, man, the point is just barely beginning!"

DOUBLES TACTICS

The first step toward playing competent doubles is to form a team. It takes at least two or three years of practicing, playing, and planning together to form a team coordinated on offense and defense. This is because of the many factors involved, such as knowing the type of shot or tactical move your partner will probably employ under a multitude of circumstances so you can optimally position yourself for the expected return, knowing who should take shots hit down the middle, diagnosing together answers for the strategy of the opposition, developing means for exploiting the weaknesses of the adversaries, encouraging one another by "talking it up," and helping judgment by calling "in," "out," and "back." Teamwork alone accounts for an estimated 25 percent of the success of a doubles combine. The most famous teams have been composed of a play maker who enticed the opponents into a weak return by finesse, fakes, teasers, and spin, or drew them out of position by well-planned maneuvers, and a rangy power player who took maximum advantage of every engineered opportunity by blasting a winner.

The service is usually designated the one most important stroke in doubles. If they can't break your serve, they can't beat you! The serving team has an offensive advantage that must be clung to tenaciously. About 30 percent of all strokes used in doubles, and 20 percent of all winning shots, are serves. Losing the offensive advantage and dropping a service game is one of the cardinal sins of doubles, as loss of service often results in the loss of a set. To make capital of the service, the stroke should force a defensive return by the receiver and permit the server to get within about fifteen feet of the net as he follows his service into the volley position. For both purposes it is best to develop a dependable American twist service that will put the first ball into play about 80 percent of the time (the server has almost twice as good a chance to win the point with a good first service as with a good second service). The preferred target for the service is deep in the receiver's backhand corner. The twist serve should be hit at about three-fourths speed to give the server control and plenty of time to get on top of the net so that he can volley a poor return of service down offensively.

The partner of the server at net must note the bounce point of the service, watch the receiver in order to anticipate the type and direction of the return of service, and then move to the proper spot to establish the best offensive formation. In general his move will be toward the center of the court. He should be prepared to poach to put away weak returns of service, and to move fast to cover effective offensive lob returns when hit over his or the advancing server's head. The net man also plays an important part in any of the numerous variations of the reverse service formations and the signaled poach plays (Figures 13 and 21).

The return of service is the most difficult shot in doubles, as evidenced by the fact that this shot sets the stage for the receiving team, which usually loses seven out of eight games. The most effective return is a low, dipping cross-court dink or top-spin drive that forces the server to volley up and permits the receiving team to move in to the net position to volley offensively. If the receiver can carry out this dual assignment, there is a tremendous payoff because he turns the odds of winning the point from two to one against him to two to one in his favor. To keep the opponents guessing, the receiver must lob occasionally and drive down the line against a poaching net man. But by all odds the most important thing is to get the ball back, as there is always the chance of a serving-team error even on the feeblest of returns. The partner of the receiver at the modified net position (near the T) should note quickly the type and direction of the return of service, glimpse any move by the opposing net man to poach, and watch the type of first volley the server is about to play. So alerted, the modified net man can often make impossible gets or drift to the center to put away weak first volleys by the server. Whenever the receiving team is in doubt, hitting low, down the middle is probably the best answer.

Net play is the thing that wins doubles matches. Remember that one third of all shots in doubles are volleys; and, excluding the service and return of service, which must be played from the back court, a staggering 80 percent of all points are won at the net position. And 80 percent of all placements are made from the net position.

Net play starts with the first volley, the most important and most difficult volley, about 85 percent of which are made by the server as he advances to the net position. The server must play this volley effectively if he is to win his service. If the return of service is high, the server must be in far enough to hit down for a placement, or at least to force a weak return that will lead to a winner on the next volley. If the return is weak enough to permit a poach, the net man should be able to knock it away for a point. Usually the server and the poacher drive weak returns at or past the opponent in the modified net position. On the other hand, if the return of service is so expertly executed as to force the server to hit up a weak volley, the receiving team should be able to move in quickly and volley down for the winner.

In almost half the cases there is no immediate winner; an intermediate situation prevails and the net-position battle is joined. The server should generally play his first volley deep down the middle if the receiver hangs back, or at his feet near the middle if he advances. Then the struggle begins to jockey the opponents out of position or to force a weak return. Whichever side of the net you are on, until you can hit a winner, make your opponents hit up. Standard strategy calls for crisp volleys to the center to draw the opponents to the middle, then an angle volley for the point; or angle volleys to open up the center for an unanswerable volley down the middle. A soft volley at the feet of the opposition will often force a volley or half volley up, so that the striking team can move in on top of the net and volley down heavily to win the point.

The net battle is so fast that good anticipation is a must.

In every phase of doubles there is almost no base-line play; a player never remains on, or retreats to, the base line unless he is forced to do so. If you find yourself marooned in the back court, you should mix up well-concealed low dinks and drives with lobs—anything to get back toward the net safely and at once.

PARTING WORDS

When you mold it all together—anticipation, tactics, stroke production, physical fitness, concentration, and determination—you will have achieved true courtcraft.

The object of the game is to win. Better yet is to win within the framework of true sportsmanship. This includes not only fair play but consideration of others—the younger players, tournament officials, your tennis association, and others who have helped to build the two great games of tennis.

Before closing, may we wish you all good bounces, perfect line calls, continued improvement in courtcraft, and, above all, increased enjoyment from tennis.

ST. LOUIS COMMUNITY
AT FLORISSANT VALLEY

LIBRARY
ST. LOUIS COMMUNITY COLLEGE
   AT FLORISSANT VALLEY

NOW KNOW YE, that I, the said Walter Clopton Wingfield, do hereby declare the nature of my said Invention, and in what manner the same is to be performed, to be particularly described and ascertained in and by the following statement, that is to say:—

The object and intention of this Invention consists in constructing a portable court by means of which the ancient game of tennis is much simplified, can be played in the open air, and dispenses with the necessity of having special courts erected for that purpose.

The manner by which I propose to accomplish the above object is as follows:—I insert two standards in the ground at about twenty-one feet from each other; between these two standards a large oblong net is stretched. To each of the said standards I attach a triangular shaped net in such a manner that the standard shall divide the said triangular net into two straight angle triangles, each of which is kept respectively at right angles to each side of the oblong net aforesaid by means of loops and strings, and is fixed to pegs driven in the ground.

The large oblong net forms the dividing wall of the court, and the triangular net the wings or side walls thereof, whilst the floor is marked out by paint, coloured cord, or tape into "in" and "out" courts, serving as crease, right and left courts, and boundaries. By this simple apparatus a portable court is obtained by means of which the old game of tennis, which has always been an indoor amusement, and which few can enjoy on account of the great expense of building a brick court, may be made an outdoor one, and placed within the reach of all, as the above-described portable court can be erected in a few minutes on a lawn, on ice, or in any suitable sized space either in or out of doors.

And in order to explain my said Invention more fully I now proceed to describe the means by which it may be carried into practical effect, reference being had to the illustrative Sheet of Drawing accompanying these Presents, and to the figures and letters of reference marked thereon, respectively as follows:—

Description of the Drawing.

Figure 1 shows a perspective view of the new and improved portable court formed by stretching an oblong net A, B, C, D, between two standards E, F, inserted in the ground; to these standards are attached the two triangular nets G, H, K, G¹, H¹, K¹, stretched by means of the ropes L.

Figure 2 shows a perspective view of the mode of stretching the